VENEZUELA

WHAT EVERYONE NEEDS TO KNOW®

VENEZUELA
WHAT EVERYONE NEEDS TO KNOW®

MIGUEL TINKER SALAS

OXFORD
UNIVERSITY PRESS

OXFORD
UNIVERSITY PRESS

Oxford University Press is a department of the University of
Oxford. It furthers the University's objective of excellence in research,
scholarship, and education by publishing worldwide.

Oxford   New York
Auckland   Cape Town   Dar es Salaam   Hong Kong   Karachi
Kuala Lumpur   Madrid   Melbourne   Mexico City   Nairobi
New Delhi   Shanghai   Taipei   Toronto

With offices in
Argentina   Austria   Brazil   Chile   Czech Republic   France   Greece
Guatemala   Hungary   Italy   Japan   Poland   Portugal   Singapore
South Korea   Switzerland   Thailand   Turkey   Ukraine   Vietnam

Oxford is a registered trademark of Oxford University Press
in the UK and certain other countries.

"What Everyone Needs to Know" is a registered trademark of
Oxford University Press.

Published in the United States of America by
Oxford University Press
198 Madison Avenue, New York, NY 10016

Cataloging-in-Publication data is on file at the Library of Congress
ISBN 978-0-19-978329-8 (hbk); 978-0-19-978328-1 (pbk)

1 3 5 7 9 8 6 4 2
Printed in the United States of America
on acid-free paper

*To Luna Isabel and Nylen Diego, may you continue
to always ask* por qué *(why)?*

CONTENTS

Part Two   Venezuela in the Twentieth Century   59

Part Three   Oil and Revolution: The Rise
of Hugo Chávez   **132**

ACKNOWLEDGMENTS

In writing this book, I am deeply indebted to the previous work of academics, intellectuals, and writers in Venezuela and the United States who have sought to interpret the complex history and society of Venezuela. Engagement with colleagues in both countries has made this work possible. In particular, I wish to acknowledge Steve Ellner, Daniel Hellinger, and T. M. Scruggs who read portions of this manuscript and provided their insights. At Pomona College, my colleagues Sidney Lemelle and Victor Silverman were always willing to read drafts and engage the subject. At Oxford, Timothy Bent, my editor, patiently guided this project to completion. I also wish to thank Keely Latchman and Alyssa O'Connell for their assistance. I am also grateful to Prabhu Chinnasamy and all those who contributed to the production of the book. *Muchas Gracias.*

Map of Venezuela

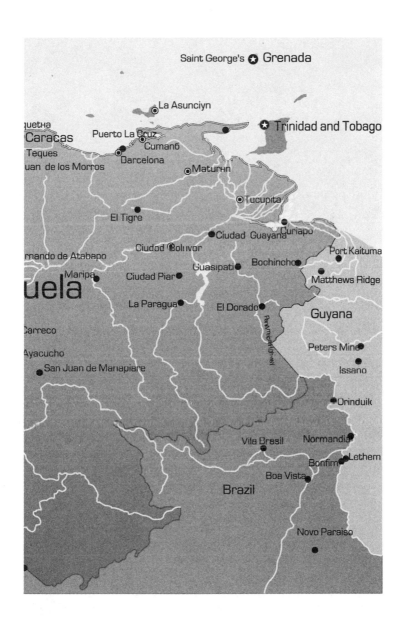

GLOSSARY

AD: Democratic Action (1941). Social Democratic Party, the leading political party after 1958.

ALBA: Bolivarian Alliance of the People of our America (2004). Includes Venezuela, Cuba, Bolivia, Ecuador, Saint Lucia, Antigua and Barbuda, Nicaragua, Dominica, Saint Vincent and the Grenadines, and El Salvador.

buhoneros: street vendors, common in most major Venezuelan cities.

CELAC: Community of Latin American and Caribbean States (2011). Consists of thirty-two member nations; does not include the United States or Canada.

CNE: National Electoral Council. An independent body established by the Constitution of 1999 to administer the electoral process.

COPEI: Committee of Independent Political Electoral Organization (1946). Christian Democratic Party.

Criollos: descendants of Spanish born in the Americas.

fueros: special colonial era privilege that exempted military from civilian tribunals.

FEDECAMARAS: Federation of Chambers of Commerce and Associations of Commerce and Production (1944).

godos: name given to conservatives who assumed power after independence.

mantuano: term used to describe a small minority of white colonial era Venezuelan elites.

mene: naturally occurring oil seeps.

MAS: Movement towards Socialism (1971). Founded by former members of the Communist Party.

MBR-200: Revolutionary Bolivarian Movement-200. Founded by Chávez (1982), evolved into the MVR, Movement of the Fifth Republic (1997).

MEP: People's Electoral Movement (1968). A political party formed by former members of AD.

MERCOSUR: Common Market of the South. Includes Brazil, Uruguay, Argentina, Paraguay, Venezuela, and Bolivia.

MIR: Movement of the Revolutionary Left (1960). Founded by former members of AD; participated in armed insurgency.

MUD: Unity Roundtable (2008). Opposition umbrella organization.

pardos: free people of color, typically African and European heritage.

PCV: Communist Party of Venezuela (1931).

PdVSA: Petroleos de Venezuela, the national Venezuela oil company.

PPT: Nation for All (1997). Left political party; part of governing coalition.

PSUV: United Socialist Party of Venezuela (2007).

SN: National Security. Repressive arm of the Pérez Jiménez dictatorship.

UNASUR: Union of South American Nations (2008). Includes all the nations of South America.

URD: Democratic Republican Union (1945). Social democratic party, member of the Pact of Punto Fijo.

VENEZUELA

WHAT EVERYONE NEEDS TO KNOW®

INTRODUCTION

The first thing most people outside of Venezuela know about the country is its former president, Hugo Rafael Chávez Frías, one of the most charismatic and controversial leaders in the Western Hemisphere in the last one hundred years, whose death in 2013 traumatized the nation. The political discontent and the support of social movements that propelled Chávez to power in 1998 thrust Venezuela onto the international stage and recast relations with the United States, Latin America, and the rest of the world. Chávez represented the first of a wave of Latin American leftist leaders to assume office during the 1990s and the early 2000s in the wake of Washington's policies that dramatically increased inequality in the region.

Venezuela's previous disengagement from regional issues and its newfound notoriety under Chávez were directly related to the vast oil reserves that sustain not only its economy but remain a central component of its culture and its very identity. Oil has served as the nexus of Venezuelan-United States relations since the discovery of vast deposits in the 1920s began to shape economic and political relations, and forged a web of personal and social relations that has endured over time.

Except for its connection to oil, before 1998 Venezuela seldom registered in the North American popular imagination. With large oil reserves and the profits they generated, economic and political elites in Venezuela did little to promote the country outside its borders. Aside from an occasional article in *National Geographic* that usually highlighted the beauty of its natural environment, the purported exceptional character of its democracy, and the importance of its oil economy, most people would be hard-pressed to find an in-depth account on Venezuela in the mainstream media or popular press.

The factors common to other Latin American nations that might have brought Venezuela to the full attention of the United States did not exist. With little or no promotion, Venezuela remained something of an undiscovered gem, never becoming a popular destination for tourists seeking warm Caribbean beaches despite its exceptional coastline, a chain of tropical islands, and spectacular offshore coastal reefs. It also was not on the itinerary of people seeking to explore indigenous civilizations or expressions of Afro-Latin American culture. Unlike the promotion of Brazil's African heritage and Mexico's indigenous traditions, through most of Venezuela's history there was no concerted effort by those in power to highlight the country's diverse racial or ethnic heritage. Its diverse environment—including snow-capped Andean mountains, vast Amazon rainforests with unique topography, windswept sand dunes, the largest fresh-water lake in South America, and the world's highest waterfall—never attracted significant numbers of foreign visitors. Few knew about its culinary traditions, its *arepas* (corn cakes) that are consumed daily, *cachápas* (corn pancakes), *pabellón* (the de facto national dish of string beef, white rice, black beans, yucca), *hallacas* (a Christmas dish similar in some ways to tamales), and many other dishes.

Immigration might have increased contact between the United States and Venezuela, as it did with other Latin American countries. However, unlike those countries, Venezuelans seldom emigrated in significant numbers to the United States or to other parts of the world. The 2000 United States Census Bureau placed the number of Venezuelans in the country at 91,507, a significant percentage of whom reside in South Florida. The 2010 census recorded that their numbers had increased to 215,023. Even accounting for an undocumented population or any recent unlisted increases, Venezuela has over thirty million people, suggesting that despite dramatic political changes, only a relatively small percentage of the population has actually emigrated to the United States. Nonetheless, Venezuelan elites and members of the upper middle class have regularly traveled to South Florida since the 1950s and have even begun to acquire property, establishing a strong presence in the Miami area. Drawn by the oil interests headquartered in the region, Venezuelans also commonly emigrated to Texas, especially Houston and Dallas. The oil industry and business interests motivated most contact between Venezuelans and North Americans.

On occasion, Venezuela's independence leader, Simón Bolívar (1783–1830) drew attention to the country. Bolívar had proposed the creation of a supra-nation composed of former Spanish colonies in order to alter the balance of power between Latin America, Europe, and the United States. His writings continue to beguile those on both the left and the right who cite him to affirm their divergent points of view. Revered in Venezuela and in many other countries in Latin America as *El Libertador*, his legacy inspired proponents of social change long before Hugo Chávez appeared on the political stage. Descriptions of Bolívar in United States as the "George Washington of Latin America" fail to capture the enormous symbolic role he continues to play in contemporary Venezuela.

There are contemporary events for which Venezuela has garnered some attention in the United States. In the sports world, Venezuelans have fielded a talented pool of baseball players, second only to the Dominicans in the major leagues. Venezuelan Miguel Cabrera, the Detroit Tigers' third baseman, was the most valuable player in the American Leagues for two consecutive years, 2012 and 2013. Others might identify the country for its uncanny ability to win Miss Universe and Miss World pageants, giving rise to a cult of beauty. In an unprecedented occurrence, Venezuelan women won two consecutive Miss Universe crowns in 2008 and in 2009 and won again in 2013. Baseball and, to a certain extent, the beauty pageant phenomenon have their roots in relations with the United States and the oil industry. The US oil companies that operated in Venezuela promoted baseball as a way to socialize workers in what they considered appropriate forms of behavior. They built stadiums, sponsored teams, and subsidized star players, helping to popularize the game among all strata of Venezuelan society. Similarly, the Valley Arriba Country Club, a facility in Caracas frequented by North Americans and Venezuelans employed in the oil industry, hosted the first celebration of a Miss Venezuela pageant in 1952. Catalina swimsuits and Pan American Airways promoted Venezuela's participation in the first Miss Universe pageant held in Long Beach, California that same year.

In the last decade, Venezuela has also gained international acclaim for the success of its national youth orchestra program known popularly as *el Sistema* (the System). Started in 1975 as the brainchild of José Antonio Abreu, the program, officially known as the *Fundación Musical Simón Bolívar* (Simón Bolívar Musical Foundation), has expanded to provide underprivileged children with training in classical music throughout the country. Musicians and conductors trained under the auspices of *el Sistema*, including Gustavo Dudamel, the celebrated conductor of the Los Angeles Philharmonic, have established international reputations in leading orchestras throughout the world.

Oil, however, remains the most identifiable image associated with Venezuela. Since its discovery in the first decades of the twentieth century, it has dominated the economy and society. On December 22, 1922, the Barroso N. 2 well on the shores of Lake Maracaibo in western Venezuela erupted, spewing 100,000 barrels a day, altering Venezuela and permanently transforming its relations with the world. By 1928, with dozens of United States and European oil companies and thousands of foreigners in the country, Venezuela became the world's second leading exporter of oil, and the first by 1935. (Venezuela is currently the fifth largest exporter of oil in the world.)

In the last decade, Venezuela's oil company Petróleos de Venezuela (PdVSA) has expanded operations in the eastern Orinoco River basin, where heavy crude deposits have increased its certified reserves to 296 billion barrels, and its recoverable reserves are estimated at 513 billion barrels, an immense quantity that surpasses the holdings of Saudi Arabia as the principal petroleum reserves in the world. Venezuela also ranks first in Latin America and eighth in the world in certified natural gas reserves with 5.5 trillion cubic meters of gas. At many levels, oil continues to be the key that helps explain and elucidate contemporary Venezuelan society, culture, and history. Control of the Venezuelan state implies control over the nation's purse strings, which overwhelmingly means oil and gas. This was the case when US oil companies operated in Venezuela, and it has been the case since the country nationalized oil in 1976.

As the principal engine of the Venezuelan economy, the immensity of petroleum assets has served to obscure social inequality and has helped create an illusion that all sectors of society share in the wealth. Like a lubricant coating the various parts of an internal combustion engine, oil literally permeates every aspect of Venezuelan society in ways that are not apparent to an outsider. Long before Chávez's first electoral victory in 1998, the key role of oil was evident in practically every arena from the absurdly low price charged for gasoline—less than five cents a gallon—to subsidies and programs that reach every sector of society, including subsidized dollars for the private sector, the funding of various social programs, higher education, transportation for students, and basic food products. Many Venezuelans consider subsidies derived from the oil industry as a birthright, and no government that hopes to remain in power has altered this arrangement. This reality inevitably heightens political tensions over control of the state, and the social policies and perspectives that determine the allocations and distribution of these important resources. This fact, more than any other, informs the conflict between the divergent political factions in Venezuela.

While there is scant knowledge of Venezuela in the United States, the opposite is not the case. Among almost all sectors of society, but especially among the middle and upper classes, as noted above, there is intimate and even personal knowledge about the United States' cultural, political, and social sensibilities. Knowledge of the "American way of life" includes broad exposure to US consumer culture, fashion, music, sports, films, diet, and the English language. Many Venezuelans understand and order their relations with the outside world from the perspective of Venezuela as an oil exporter that services the energy needs of the United States.

Furthermore, the special relationship with the United States has influenced a strain of thought among middle and upper classes that Venezuela represents an exception to the experience of other Latin America countries. Sustained relations with United States oil interests, government policy, and the presence of foreigners in the country has shaped social and political attitudes as well as consumer patterns. Without having to exercise an actual physical presence, at many levels the United States and the lifestyle it promotes functions as an internal constituent within the Venezuelan sociopolitical landscape.

Efforts by the Chávez government and the social movements that elected him to promote a brand of twenty-first century socialism have occurred within a country where the prevailing values of a capitalist society have sunk deep roots. The export model that the oil industry engendered led many social sectors to develop faith in the tenets of the capitalist system, a free market, the importance of private property, and a strong sense of individualism.

Oil revenue appeared to transform Venezuela, and nowhere was this more evident than in Caracas. Leaving behind its quaint tradition of identifying addresses by their proximity to street corners and an urban landscape dotted by red tile roofs, within the span of decades the city became a metropolis of skyscrapers and bustling freeways. To a lesser extent, this transformation also occurred throughout the country in the leading cities, including Maracaibo, Valencia, Maracay, Maturin, and Barcelona. Beyond a physical transformation, Venezuelans increasingly appeared to lose a connection to their immediate past.

By the mid-1950s, Caracas and Maracaibo, the country's two largest cities, boasted United States-inspired department stores and supermarkets that catered to the expanding tastes of middle-class Venezuelans. These and other practices aimed at stimulating consumerism spawned a lasting legacy of conspicuous consumption. Rates of electrical consumption in Venezuela, for instance, place it as one of the highest per capita consumers of energy in the region. With forty-two percent of Venezuelans claiming to drink Scotch whiskey, the country has the highest per capita consumption rate of this beverage in Latin America, especially the eighteen-year-old variety. It has one of the highest per capita rates of beer consumption in the region with over 89.95 liters per inhabitant. Twitter usage is among the highest in the world, Chávez, who had close to four million followers, regularly used the medium to reach a broad audience. Likewise, per capita ownership of smartphones surpasses many other countries in Latin America.

To comprehend Venezuelan political and social values, it is essential to consider the role the oil industry has played in generating expectations for continued growth and social mobility. Foreign control of the oil industry for much of the twentieth century reinforced these values. Nationalization raised expectations that the country would eventually attain levels of development similar to those of other more advanced Western nations. It is hard to underestimate the spell that oil cast over the nation, both in the immense profits the elites derived and the privileged lifestyle enjoyed by those employed in the industry.

The Chávez phenomenon

Writing about contemporary Venezuela today is a complicated task, one made all the more difficult as we assess the post-Chávez landscape, a landscape that he shaped more profoundly than any leader in Latin America in this century. A country that previously seldom registered on the world stage became the source of global attention, mostly centered on the actions of Chávez, who died in March 2013. Informed by media accounts, many people seem to hold relatively one-sided opinions of Venezuela under Chávez. Typically depicting Venezuela as the principal nemesis of the United States in the region, most media accounts usually began their coverage by portraying Chávez as a faithful protégé of Fidel Castro, hoping to capitalize on a reservoir of enmity toward the Cuban revolution. Reducing Venezuela to a conspiratorial regional left bloc, many unfamiliar with Latin America's distinct national histories are quick to claim that Evo Morales, the president of Bolivia, and Rafael Correa, the president of Ecuador, were walking in lockstep with Chávez—a kind of leftist "three amigos" cannily conspiring against the United States.

Venezuela's newfound prominence reflects the extent to which the country has managed to insert itself into regional and world affairs in little over a decade, influencing international debates on a wide range of topics. Much of what Venezuela has proposed—including a nationalist energy policy, multipolar international relations, regional integration, food security, and national sovereignty—now frame mainstream political discourse throughout Latin America. Undoubtedly Venezuela's huge oil reserves have served to magnify its importance across the globe. Venezuela's newfound presence on the international stage is even more dramatic precisely because of its previous disengagement not just from regional concerns but from world matters.

Accustomed to dealing with a country that operated firmly in its orbit, the Washington political establishment, the media, and many academics in the United States appeared ill-prepared to deal with the dramatic changes that gained momentum in Venezuela after 1998. In the past Venezuelan politicians seldom ventured from travel between Caracas and Washington, occasionally visiting New York and the United Nations, but never including Beijing, Moscow, Brasilia, Buenos Aires, and much less Tehran or Luanda, Angola on their itinerary. Now they do so frequently. Although the United States is still an important market for its oil, Venezuela no longer privileges relations with Washington, and instead promotes ties and pursues investments from countries as distinct as Brazil, India, Iran, Russia, and China.

The so-called Chávez phenomenon, however captivating, is not necessarily the best way to understand contemporary Venezuela. While it would be relatively simple to divide Venezuela into periods that correspond to before and after Chávez's first electoral victory (and to adopt the US media fixation with controversial figures), the actions of one person who was in power a little over a decade do not do justice to the history of the country. Oil and the political, economic, and social expectations it generated provides a much more comprehensive lens through which to understand contemporary Venezuela. This book therefore explores Venezuela from the perspective of periods before and after the rise of the oil economy. The first part of the book traces the historical continuities between the colonial period and the rise of an independent yet fragmented nation. It highlights Venezuela's torturous transition to a republic during the nineteenth century, marked by recurring civil wars and the absence of a powerful national elite capable of imposing a unifying national project. Breaking with traditional interpretations, this section underscores the role of race and inequality as constant sources of social and political tension in the country.

The second part of the book turns to the twentieth century. The discovery of oil in the first decades of the twentieth century held out the promise of dramatic change, although in practice it did little to alter the structures of power or the nature of economic relations. Rather than introduce a new anticipated modern era, the oil industry grafted itself onto the long dictatorship of Juan Vicente Gómez (1908–1935). The nascent oil industry lent Gómez legitimacy while simultaneously extracting generous concessions for its own accumulation of economic and political power. The Venezuelan economy increasingly became dependent on oil revenues, and imported much of what it consumed. In fact, by 1935 Venezuela was a net importer of basic foodstuffs.

In the decade after the death of Gómez, divergent visions of the country emerged. For many in Venezuela, the government of Isaías Medina Angarita (1941–1945) held out the hope for an alternative form of development, one that would foment agriculture and promote a Venezuelan industrial sector. A civilian-military coup in October 1945 put an end to that hope. The short-lived democratic experiment that followed ended in yet another military government that lasted, with some changes, from 1948 until January 1958.

Despite its connections to antidemocratic regimes, oil unleashed new political forces and expectations that military governments proved unable to control. The late 1950s produced renewed clashes between middle-class political parties, leftist groups championing the lower socioeconomic strata of the nation, and the military in power. With the ouster of the last military dictator, Marcos Pérez Jiménez, in 1958, democratic parties devised a power-sharing arrangement to minimize interparty conflict, control the military, and limit challenges from the left that had played a decisive role in overthrowing the dictatorship. After 1958, the two parties that dominated the political landscape, Acción Democrática or AD (Democratic Action, Social Democrats) and the Comité de Organización Política Electoral Independiente or COPEI (Committee of Political Electoral Independent Organization—Christian Democrats) used a carrot-and-stick approach: oil revenues were used to build patronage networks aimed at the middle classes and create social programs to mitigate the plight of the poorer sectors with the expectation of their votes at election time. Any demands for more wealth sharing from the left were severely repressed. This arrangement served the government well until oil prices declined precipitously in the late 1980s. Repeated charges of corruption, cronyism, mismanagement of the economy, and the crash of several leading banks and insurance companies deepened the political crisis. Oil revenues had initially allowed Venezuela to avoid the austerity measures that had produced crisis in Mexico, Argentina, and other Latin American countries during the 1980s. Facing worsening conditions, the AD government, after first promising exactly the opposite in the elections of 1988, capitulated to international lending agencies and introduced austerity measures that sparked widespread political unrest and created the conditions that gave rise to a new alternative.

Finally, the book's third section focuses on the Chávez era and, now, the post-Chávez era. As a major producer of oil within OPEC, Venezuela remains important to the United States and the countries of Latin America. After more than a decade of social transformation it is difficult to imagine a scenario under which it will revert to the two-party/single policy form of electoral democracy that the United States still promotes within the region. To win support among the poor in the past few years, conservative opposition leaders have moderated their rhetoric and habitually promise to continue supporting social programs that mitigate inequality.

Despite depictions to the contrary, social movements and groups that supported Chávez and now his successor Nicolás Maduro are not undiscerning masses blindly captivated by charismatic leadership. Their loyalty depends on the ability of the government to fulfill its promise of political and socio-economic change and improve their standard of living. The social forces unleashed in the last decades have gained a new voice and will demand a continued role in society. Likewise, it is unlikely that the well-organized opposition to the government will retreat or cease to defend their interests. When oil was discovered in Venezuela, the population hovered at 2.5 million people; today the country has surpassed thirty million inhabitants. Idyllic depictions of the past fail to capture the dramatic increase in population and the new social and economic demands that this generates for any government in power.

To say that Venezuela today is polarized is tantamount to a cliché. Politics has divided families and strained friendships. However, to suggest that class and racial divisions did not exist before the election of Chávez fails to recognize the deep social and racial fissures that have existed throughout the entire course of Venezuela history. What is clear though is that the appearance of Chávez on the political stage served to channel economic and social discontent that might have otherwise degenerated into open conflict as occurred previously in the *Caracazo*, the social rebellion of February 1989 that engulfed the capital and other cities.

Dueling political, social, and even cultural visions fuel the current polarization. Chávez and the dramatic changes underway since 1999 profoundly challenged deeply held individual and group assumptions about Venezuelan society, including political alliances, class and social relations, national identity, racial constructions, and even Venezuela's place in the world. Upper- and middle-class sectors, long accustomed to privileged relations with the state and civic society, fear that new political arrangements and social programs come at their expense. In reality the many new social programs are new parallel structures and have not directly affected the wealthy, and in fact some have benefitted economically from the policies of the past decade.

However, the conservative opposition's concerns are much deeper than simply politics or economics. Many sectors presumed that oil permitted Venezuela to claim a distinct status within Latin America, and considered natural its relative isolation from the rest of Latin America. For many, the election of Chávez meant that Venezuela became everything they had attempted to negate: another Latin American country led by a mixed-race, charismatic ex-military officer that promised to improve conditions for the poor, and worse, dared to invite them to participate as full-fledged citizens of the newly conceptualized nation.

Members of the current opposition often complain that they have "lost their country," and hope to recover the old Venezuela. This perspective, at its core, reflects their sense of ownership over a national project that embodied their values and affirmed their position in society. Many of these values embody a vision of Venezuela as an oil-producing nation aligned with the United States and Western values. The growing population, formerly marginalized and largely absent from this previous national narrative, has, for the moment, lent its support to political forces offering an alternative reading of Venezuelan society. Social movements, some with a long history of struggle and others newly empowered, demand to be included in the political process and share the nation's oil wealth. Whatever government holds power in Caracas will have to deal with this new political reality. How these dueling forces resolve these contending visions of Venezuela has significant political and economic implications for the United States and the rest of the globe.

Since Venezuela seldom attracted attention in previous decades, scholars in the United States who studied the country labored on the margins of a field dominated by Mexico and the Southern Cone, referring to southern Brazil, Argentina, Chile, Paraguay, and Uruguay—the most prosperous macro-region in South America. But recent political upheavals, as exemplified by Cuba after Fidel Castro, or Nicaragua after the Sandinistas, sparked renewed interest in those countries whose earlier challenges to United States policy had already generated an upsurge in scholarly interest. As was previously the case with Cuba and Nicaragua, Venezuela has been transformed from a friendly ally into an obstacle to Washington's plans for the hemisphere. This adversarial relationship has prompted scholars to question the operating assumptions that existed about the country's history and society, and new scholarship is emerging that offers a more nuanced view of the country's past and present.

The media—more than just *National Geographic*—is also drawn by the events that are reshaping the country. Increased coverage, however, does not always produce greater clarity and is often unable to explain either the intricate nuances of Venezuelan society or the complex web of personal and economic relations that drive politics. Seldom is there any serious attempt to move beyond the dueling forces of Chávez and the leadership of the opposition bloc that challenged his presidency and now his legacy. This book seeks to redirect that conversation.

Part One

VENEZUELA BEFORE OIL

*What groups lived in Venezuela before the arrival of the
Spaniards in the sixteenth century?*

With its unpredictable weather patterns, fragmented topography, and impenetrable rainforest, Venezuela proved incapable of sustaining large complex and hierarchical structured
indigenous societies similar to those found in Mexico, Central
America, or the Andes. Its geography not only accentuated
physical boundaries but also cultural frontiers among groups
that inhabited the expansive coastal regions and its valleys,
the Andean mountain range, and the dense tropical rainforest
and Orinoco delta region.

Venezuela's first inhabitants, descendants of ethnic groups
with roots in the greater Amazon region, primarily *Caribes*
(Caribs) and *Arahuacos* (Arawaks) in the east and central
valleys and from the *Chibchas* (*Timote-Cuica*) in the western
Andes, represented rich cultural and social traditions, speak-
ing multiple languages and never constituting a single unified polity. For many indigenous groups originating in the
Brazilian Amazon, Venezuela also served as a point of transit
on migratory paths en route to the islands of the Caribbean.
These groups exhibited varied levels of development. Hunters,
fishing people, and gatherers such as the Warao of the delta
thrived at the same time as groups such as the Chibcha in

the Andes, who lived in fixed communities, had developed irrigation systems, and produced squashes, maize, potatoes, and a wide variety of other tubers. A hereditary *cacique*, with varying degrees of authority, or a council of elders served as de facto leaders for most communities. Their spiritual world included worship of the earth, sun, moon, wind, and water, elements that influenced their physical world and dictated the agricultural calendar.

Influenced by strong positivist views during the nineteenth century and subsequently a vision of Western modernity that largely dismissed the past, indigenous groups, until recently, seldom entered into the Venezuelan national consciousness. They are found in popular culture as symbolic figures encountered by the Spanish when they colonized Venezuela in the early part of the sixteenth century. Grammar school texts and popular literature focused on the deeds of a handful of *caciques* (indigenous leaders) such as Guaicaipuro, Chacao, Naiguata, Baruta, Tamanaco, Tiuna, and Yaracuy, who battled the Spaniards as they attempted to conquer the central coast and adjacent valleys. Their deeds, the subject of much official mythmaking, percolated in popular folklore, obscuring the reality experienced by the local indigenous peoples that encountered the Europeans. The names of these mythical *caciques* serve to identify states, cities, towns, military garrisons, and even a major international hotel in Caracas.

During the colonial period, which began in 1498 with the arrival of the Spaniards and ended in 1811 when Venezuela proclaimed independence, royal authorities assigned *resguardos* (communally owned Indian lands) where the indigenous populations could maintain some level of autonomy from *criollos* (people of mixed Spanish heritage born in the Americas). As in other regions of Latin America, the term "Indian" became synonymous with the tribute the crown expected the indigenous groups to provide.

After independence, *criollos* altered the indigenous relations with the state. Under the guise of incorporating indigenous peoples into postcolonial society, they began the process of privatizing previously held communal lands. Authorities and landed interests often sought to classify indigenous lands as *terrenos baldíos* (vacant lands) subject to auction. Native Americans that resided close to established settlements or near productive landed estates faced greater social pressure and direct encroachments of their land. By the 1880s the government abolished the term "indigenous" except for its application to communities that resided in the region of the Amazon basin or the northwestern border with Colombia.

Currently indigenous groups formally account for between two and three percent of the Venezuelan population, the largest groups being the Wayúu, Warao, Pemon, and Añu. Most indigenous communities inhabit areas along the border with Colombia in the area of the peninsula of the Guajira in western Venezuela and in the country's vast Amazon region and Orinoco river delta. As a result, it is not surprising that many Venezuelans continue to view the existence of Indians largely as a frontier issue, not a central component of social or cultural life. Though many mixed-race Venezuelans possess significant indigenous lineage, few identify with this heritage; only in recent years has a Native American descent generated pride. Indigenous groups continue to be marginalized in and by Venezuelan society.

What is the origin of the name "Venezuela"?

Along with many parts of the country's history, Venezuela's name remains the subject of controversy. Traditionally, every grammar school child in Venezuela learned that European cartographers and explorers who mapped the area in 1499 inspired the country's name. According to this story, an expedition led by Alfonso Ojeda and including Juan de la Cosa and Amerigo Vespucci sailed between the Peninsula Paria in eastern Venezuela and the Peninsula of la Guajira, passing by the entrance of Lake Maracaibo near an area known as Sinamaica. The presence of the olive-skinned indigenous Añu (Arawak: "People of the Water") and their thatched palm-covered residences erected on wooden poles over the lake purportedly reminded Vespucci of constructions in Venice.

For the Indians, hoping to escape poisonous snakes and swarms of mosquitoes, building over the lake made sense. Just as important, the lake was an important source of food, providing fish and an assortment of fowl. Water transportation also connected them to communities around the lakeshore with whom they traded. Despite Vespucci's claim, cartographer de la Cosa is credited with using the term "little Venice" on a map he sketched after visiting the area. By 1528, the name "Venezuela" appeared on a map utilized by the Spanish crown to cede control of the territory to the Welsers, a German banking and merchant family which, in searching for the fabled *El Dorado*, pillaged most of northwestern Venezuela and left a trail of devastation.

"Venezuela" has also been attributed to the indigenous Añu who inhabited the area. According to this interpretation, which ironically also relies on Spanish sources, Martín Fernández de Enciso recorded "Veneçiuela" in a 1519 publication, attributing the name to the Indians of the region for whom it meant "large body of water." Other Spanish officials who referred to the area by its indigenous name subsequently confirmed this interpretation. What is beyond dispute is that the Hispanized term "Venezuela," first used to describe indigenous communities only in the northwestern region, eventually expanded in usage to identify the entire area of the modern nation-state.

How did Spanish colonial rule mark Venezuela?

Christopher Columbus disembarked in eastern Venezuela on his third voyage in August of 1498, landing at a site settled by the Karina indigenous people on the eastern Peninsula de

Paria, across from the island of Trinidad. The nation's mythology has incorporated Columbus's lavish accounts of having discovered an "earthly paradise" and "land of grace" as well as subsequent portrayals of Venezuela as the new *El Dorado*. Although he reconnoitered the entrance to the Orinoco River, Columbus's ships proved unable to navigate the strong currents. Perhaps his inability to explore further inland contributed to his lifelong ignorance that he had reached continental South America.

Efforts to conquer Venezuela met with stiff indigenous resistance, much of it prompted by Spanish campaigns to capture Indian slaves to replace those killed by disease and conflict on other settled Caribbean islands or to send them to Panama, where they would be forced to transport goods across the isthmus. Attempts to colonize eastern Venezuela beginning in 1506 and western Venezuela in 1527 ended in failure, producing few permanent settlements aside from the city of Coro in the state of Falcón. Other efforts at colonization included an experiment in 1521 by the Dominican friar Bartolome de las Casas, who advocated a peaceful colonization of the region, but the settlement nonetheless succumbed to indigenous resistance and opposition by Spanish colonists.

By the late 1720s, the Spanish crown authorized the Welsers and other Spanish colonists to import African slaves to work in mines and various agricultural enterprises. Some scholars have estimated that upwards of 100,000 enslaved Africans arrived in Venezuela during the Spanish colonial period. The numbers of African slaves may in fact have been higher, since there is evidence that slaves were brought in from Colombia and ports in the Caribbean. Throughout the sixteenth and seventeenth centuries, landowners regularly submitted requests to Spanish authorities to import additional slaves, claiming to need laborers to expand operations. Although enslaved Africans participated in multiple economic activities including mining, agriculture, pearl diving, and as cowboys and sailors, increasingly they became the principal source of labor to grow and harvest cacao (the cacao bean is used to make chocolate), colonial Venezuela's principal agricultural export. Cacao production in Venezuela became synonymous with African slavery much the same way as sugar did on the islands of the Caribbean. For the *criollo* elite, owning a cacao plantation operated by slaves became a sign of distinction in colonial society. Although used earlier, by the nineteenth century the designation of *gran cacao* (great cacao producer) served to describe a person of wealth. Cacao production proliferated in the fertile central valleys in and around Barlovento in the state of Miranda, center to some of the highest-quality cacao produced in Venezuela. As a result, a significant number of Afro-Venezuelans resided in Barlovento and it remains today a symbolic and cultural center of the African presence in Venezuela.

Most cacao plantations and the slaves that worked the fields occupied coastal central states such as Miranda and Aragua where the great majority of Venezuela's population resided. The African presence and heritage, however, extended throughout Venezuela, including the Lake Maracaibo region, the Andes highlands, the *llanos* (plains), the eastern region that faced the Caribbean, and the state of Bolívar. On multiple occasions, slaves escaped the oppressive conditions they encountered and with others formed independent communities known in Venezuela as *cumbes* and *rochelas*—settlements of freed African and mixed-race individuals. Slave rebellions and indigenous resistance occurred frequently throughout the colonial period.

After having consolidated a foothold in the west in Falcón and in the east on the Peninsula de Paria, the Spanish began to colonize central Venezuela, formally establishing the city of Santiago de Leon de Caracas in 1567 on the site of a previous settled *hato*, a small cattle ranch. Surrounded by fertile valleys, a comfortable climate, and access to a nearby port, Caracas enjoyed many economic advantages and by 1576 it had become the administrative capital of colonial Venezuela.

Although the Spanish stumbled onto natural oil seeps and vast tar beds, at the time they had no commercial value. Efforts at using crude oil as a remedy for a variety of ailments proved futile. On the other hand, the colonizers quickly depleted pearl beds on the coastal islands of Cubagua and Margarita, devastating the environment and decimating the indigenous population.

With no evident gold or silver deposits, and few indigenous people to convert or enslave, the province of Venezuela remained largely on the margins of the Spanish empire. Lightly populated, it endured as six distinct provinces until 1717, when Spanish authorities joined Colombia, Ecuador, and Venezuela to form the Viceroyalty of New Granada. Bureaucrats in Bogota and Santo Domingo intermittently managed Venezuela until 1777, when the Crown created the Captaincy General of Venezuela which encompasses the modern day territory. The legacy of colonial rule gave rise to discrete regions existing largely in isolation from each other. Eastern Venezuela and the plains remained a distant outpost trading mostly with the British-controlled island of Trinidad, the central valleys interacted with the provincial capital Caracas, and in the west, Maracaibo connected the Andean mountains with trade networks reaching into the Caribbean.

A colonial export economy took shape in the late eighteen century, focusing on mining, indigo, coffee, hides, and, increasingly, cacao beans. Economic activity exhibited regional characteristics, with coffee production centered in the west, among the Andean mountain range and the piedmont region; cattle production flourishing in the expansive *llanos* and eastern plains; and cacao and dyes produced in the central valleys. The quality of Venezuelan cacao gained renown and found markets in Europe and in Mexico. Isolated from one another, many cacao-producing valleys had direct access to seaports for the export of their product. Other producers, lacking adequate infrastructure, relied mainly on either riverine systems or lake and coastal shipping to export their products.

Subsequent conflicts in post-independence Venezuela were fueled by regional elites that sought to protect their profitable agricultural interests.

What was the character of race relations in colonial society?

A pronounced racial hierarchy that sought to ensure the continuity of land ownership, social status, and privileges shaped the contours of Venezuelan colonial society. Despite the limited number of Europeans, their socioeconomic dominance ensured that a white aesthetic prevailed and hopes for social ascendancy were linked to embracing their cultural mores and shared norms. To preserve their ranks, white elites practiced endogamy, subjecting young girls to early marriage to protect family property and social standing. Colonial society consisted of a small number of Spanish administrators who monopolized high political offices and filled the ranks of the merchant class, and a few thousand *criollos* who, according to one study, accounted for less than 0.5 percent of the colonial population.

Miscegenation produced a large number of free people of mixed race, including *mestizos*, the byproduct of intermixing between Europeans and the indigenous population, and *pardos*, generally referring to people with African and European heritage. The mere existence of free *pardos* and *mestizos* in this colonial society served as a testament that, when it came to matters of sex, Spanish and *criollo* male elites did not seem to be bothered by skin color.

With a smaller indigenous population, miscegenation in Venezuela more closely resembled the racial experience of the Caribbean and Brazil, not that of Mexico or Peru. Regional variations existed in such areas such as the Andes and *llanos* where larger numbers of *mestizos* resided. Elsewhere, as the numbers of *pardos* increased, they played a significant role in society as members of militias, artisans, lawyers, professionals, and other occupations; however, racism, intertwined with the *pardos'* continued association with the legacy of slavery, limited opportunities. Colonial society included a significant number of indigenous and African slaves, but the bulk of slaves were Africans. *Criollos* owned most of the land that produced cacao and by extension benefitted directly from the exploitation of African slave labor.

The *criollos*, referred to locally as *mantuanos* because of the lace garments worn by elite women, accentuated their European heritage to affirm their social status, though increasingly indigenous and African ancestry entered their lineage. Those with mixed European lineage or more recent arrivals, known as *blancos de la orrilla* (literally, "whites from the edge") also competed for status. Living amid a vastly numerically mixed race population, the handful of *mantuano* families—related by kinship, marriage, fictive kin or business relations—exercised power through the town council in Caracas, the center of power and the largest city. When the Spanish crown in 1795 promoted a royal decree known as *Cédula Gracias al Sacar* (literally "License to Extract") allowing *pardos* to purchase a new ethnic standing and compete for much-sought-after positions, the *criollo* elite expressed alarm and sought to prevent the implementation of the proclamation, fearing that it would diminish their power.

Compounding *criollo* fears were concerns that educated *pardos* would make use of legal and social channels to subvert the racial policies that excluded them from seizing the reins of power within colonial society. For instance, Juan German Roscio, a *pardo* attorney, had gained a reputation defending mixed-race individuals in colonial tribunals. One of his most famous cases in 1797 involved a *parda*, Inés María Páez, married to a *mantuano*, Juan José Ochoa. Tired of soiling her dress in church when she kneeled, she dared to take a small rug to services, a practice reserved as a sign of distinction for elite white women. Furious at this transgression, church officials questioned the legitimacy of her marriage to Ochoa. Roscio mounted a vigorous defense to prove the legitimacy of Páez's marriage and affirmed her rights to use the rug. Concerns over such possible racial conflict pervaded colonial society, influencing the course of the wars of independence and much of the post-independent era.

What was colonial society like for women?

Although the colonial system sought to preserve patriarchal privileges centered on status and honor, it did not necessarily preclude women from exercising important roles in society. The idealized norms of the patriarchal society did not always reflect the actual lived experiences of most men and women. Women from all social backgrounds participated in colonial society, were involved directly or indirectly in politics as protagonists in social mobilizations, and contributed at multiple levels to economic, cultural, and religious life. Influenced by emerging liberal ideas, the decades before and after independence witnessed renewed activity by women to assert their rights. Recent scholarship has documented how women made use of legal tribunals to expand the discourse of citizenship claiming rights previously exercised only by men.[1] On many occasions, they filed lawsuits to protect their property, divorce or abandon abusive husbands, enforce contracts, including promises to marry, and exert control over their children. Slaves and women of color also made use of the courts to assert their rights or to enforce their freedom when others attempted to enslave them. After independence and throughout the nineteenth century, women continued to make use of local tribunals and other venues to exercise their rights and defend their status.

In cities such as Caracas, where female-headed households proved common, women from lower socioeconomic sectors served as washers, bakers, seamstresses, and cooks. Women participated directly or in support roles in many preindependence struggles that challenged the political order, including the *Comuneros* revolt (1781), the *Chirinos* rebellions

(1795–1796) and that led by Gual and España (1797). Records of the *Coro* rebellion of 1795 show that authorities targeted several slave women for severe punishment, claiming they had participated in the insurrection.

What sparked the independence movement?

Similar to colonial society throughout the Americas, early nineteenth century Venezuela was riven by a host of social cleavages. *Mantuano* elites resented the heavy hand of Spanish authorities that excluded them from high government positions and economic decision making. Some still resented the crown's earlier decisions to allow a Basque company to monopolize the sale of cacao, giving them undue political influence over the internal affairs of the province. *Criollo* refusals to accept *pardos* and free blacks on equal footing increased tensions between these groups. Burdened by *criollo* landowners, slaves and the indigenous failed to see any benefit in common ground with their oppressors.

By the last decade of the nineteenth century, multiple groups began to act on their grievances. In 1795, in the western state of Falcón, black slaves, free people of color, and indigenous groups led by José Leonardo Chirinos and José Caridad González rebelled, demanding the abolition of slavery, an end to the collection of Indian tributes, and a break from Spain. Slaves at Cariaco, in eastern Venezuela and in the central state of Guarico, rebelled a few years later. In 1797, colonial officials at the port city of La Guaira uncovered a plot by *criollos* Manuel Gual and José María España, whose political program called for an end to Spanish rule and, significantly, affirmed the rights of all Venezuelans, regardless of race. In Maracaibo, *pardos* and other mixed race people also sought to form an autonomous government in 1798. In all of these cases, Spanish authorities acted ruthlessly, killing the leaders of the insurrection, sending a clear message that they would not tolerate sedition.

After the Haitian Revolution of 1804 (an uprising by slaves and their allies that defeated the French) calls for racial equality and social change generated profound fear among *criollo* elites, who had a tenuous hold on power. Although they desired to control their own destiny, fear of revolution, especially sharing power with *pardos* and other people of color, divided *criollos* who otherwise might have favored autonomy or even independence. These divisions undermined future efforts at independence. In 1806 Francisco Miranda, a Venezuelan who had participated in the French Revolution and envisioned a united Latin America, spearheaded an expedition in April and again in August of 1806. He led a multinational force that included Venezuelans, British, and North Americans that failed to generate support among the local populace, including slaves in western Venezuela. Although these rebellions demonstrated high levels of discontent and some actually contained an alternative vision for the nation's future, it is problematic to weave them into a single narrative in favor of independence. Rather they represented disconnected and at times opposing views about the future of Venezuela.

In 1808, French forces invaded the Iberian Peninsula and forced King Charles IV's abdication of the throne, an action immediately followed by renewed calls for autonomous rule. On April 19, 1810, Caracas municipal authorities openly rejected the authority of the Spanish Captain General and he left Venezuela. To govern a newly independent Venezuela, political forces needed to control Caracas, yet interior provinces resented the economic and political privileges the capital enjoyed.

Overcoming the provinces' trepidations, by July 5, 1811, supporters of independence convinced the majority of delegates gathered at the congress in Caracas to support a formal break from Spain. A delegation that included a young Simón Bolívar and the intellectual Andres Bello travelled to London but failed to garner British recognition for Venezuelan independence. As they neared the end of their deliberations, to expand their base of support *criollos* found it necessary to make political and even social concessions to the *pardo* majority. Leading *pardos* such as Juan Germán Roscio and José Félix Ribas took part in the independence debates, and Roscio helped draft the declaration of independence. The record of their deliberations, however, reveals their unwillingness to relinquish any political power to other social sectors. Delegates made it a point to preserve the institution of slavery, which had exploited thousands of Africans, and to continue extracting tributes from Indians. The Faustian bargain on race relations failed to placate either *criollos* or *pardos* and racial divisions continued to bedevil Venezuelan society.

Why did the first movement for independence fail?

The apparent unity forged in Caracas in 1810 and subsequent independence in 1811 proved short-lived. Within weeks several provinces withdrew their support, and Venezuela was plunged into a civil war that, by 1812, ended the first independent experiment in South America. For Venezuela, independence reflected as much a civil war between social classes and racial groups as it did a conflict with Spain. Indeed, the first attempt at independence, a period known as *la Patria Boba* (roughly "the foolish republic") exposed divisions between *criollos* and the extent to which independence failed to incorporate the majority of the racially mixed population.

A second attempt at forming an independent republic (1813–1814) also ended in failure. Royalist forces led by José Tomas Boves gained the support of mixed race Venezuelans, especially *llaneros* (plainsmen), who formed an "infernal legion" of cavalrymen that overran republican forces. Boves' own history reveals the contradictory nature of desires for independence from Spain and hopes of freedom from racial and class oppression. A native of Asturias, Boves arrived in Venezuela in the employ of a commercial house. He skillfully manipulated long-standing racial animosity in Venezuela and stoked fears among the white minority that they faced the potential of another Haiti. Simón Bolívar, the emerging commander of the independence movement, also sought to polarize the conflict and declared a "war to the death" pronouncing "Spaniards and Canary islanders anticipate death, even if you are indifferent . . ." Boves matched Bolívar's cruelty, waging war without taking prisoners; the ensuing bloodbath left thousands of Venezuelans dead.

Differences among independence commanders—in this case Bolívar and the commander of eastern forces, Santiago Marino—weakened the patriots' cause. Fearing the onslaught of Boves' army on the capital, residents fled Caracas and sought refuge in eastern Venezuela. By late 1814, with patriot forces reduced to several outposts in the east, Bolívar fled the country and sought refuge in Jamaica and later Haiti. In Jamaica, Bolívar drafted his now-famous "Letter from Jamaica," formulating his vision for a united Gran Colombia comprised of Ecuador, Colombia, and Venezuela, and proposed a meeting that would bring together the independent nations of the Americas.

In May of 1816, with aid from Haiti, Bolívar and other independence leaders once again landed troops in eastern Venezuela, where they attempted to attract support by promising to free slaves who joined their movement. They were unsuccessful, and easily overwhelmed. Routed and facing challenges to his leadership, Bolívar once again fled to Haiti. In his absence, other independence leaders, including the llanero José Antonio Paéz, the pardo Manuel Piar, and the Scot Gregor MacGregor fought against the Spaniards in the plains and eastern Venezuela.

Piar presents an interesting case. The son of a Canary islander and an Afro-Curaçao mother, he waged several successful campaigns that assured the patriots a base of operations in southeastern Venezuela. Piar, like Boves, exemplified how questions of racial equality and class status plagued the independence movement. Piar's success earned him the enmity of other *criollo* revolutionary leaders, however, who never considered him their equal. This hostility became a factor when Piar challenged Bolívar's leadership upon his return to Venezuela in December of 1816.

Dreading a repeat of Haiti and the Spanish willingness to manipulate racial tensions, Bolívar feared that Piar would rally support among nonwhite sectors, weaken *criollo* resolve, and subvert his leadership of the independence process. Bolívar had Piar arrested and a council of war condemned him to death for insubordination and desertion, a decision that, for many, tarnished Bolívar's record on racial relations. Defenders insist that he accepted the decision to prevent division in the independence process and preserve his leadership. Critics condemn his actions as a clear message to *pardos* and other people of color that he would not tolerate political appeals based on race and would protect *criollos'* social position. *Criollos* in Venezuela still feared that by mobilizing *pardos*, slaves, and Indians, the independence struggle could degenerate into a race war. Race and the possibility of a racial and class conflict haunted the independence struggle and the republics that emerged after the ouster of the Spanish.

Acknowledged as the dominant leader of the independence process, Bolívar, along with his allies, oversaw a new congress at the town of Angostura in 1819 that established the political framework for a united Venezuela and Colombia, the former Spanish Colonial Viceroyalty of New Granada. Bolívar set his sights on Bogota, the political capital of the Viceroyalty that also included Ecuador. As the congress deliberated, forces commanded by Bolívar marched across southern Venezuela, crossing plains and the snow-capped Andes Mountains, where he lost hundreds of soldiers before reaching Colombia.

The battle of Boyacá sealed the defeat of the royalist forces in Colombia and Bolívar entered Bogota triumphantly on August 10, 1819. Even as he emerged victorious in Colombia, delegates at Angostura challenged Bolívar's authority and Colombian patriots viewed him with suspicion. The defeat of the Spaniards at Boyacá opened the door to taking the fight back to Venezuela and on June 24, 1821, independent forces defeated the Spaniards at the battle of Carabobo. By 1823, other victories in Colombia and at the port of Maracaibo formally confirmed Venezuela's independence. The human cost was extremely high: by the conclusion of the wars of independence, Venezuela had lost approximately a third of its population.

Inspired by his continental vision to free all of Latin America from Spanish rule, Bolívar and his allies organized troops to pursue the independence struggle in Ecuador, where in May of 1822 they defeated the Spanish at the battle of Pichincha and subsequently in Peru at the battle of Ayacucho in 1824. Even before the defeat of the Spanish, the independence congress gathered in Cúcuta, Colombia in 1821 set into motion Bolívar's dream of forming the Gran Colombia. For Bolívar, unification of the region proved more challenging than defeating the Spanish. Reflecting on this situation, he acknowledged that he feared peace more than war, since the Spanish would be defeated soon, but divisions among Latin Americans persisted.

Why is the figure of Simón Bolívar so important and what is his legacy in Venezuela?

Military leaders, many with regional support and demonstrating more battlefield prowess than Bolívar, had filled the ranks of Venezuela's independence movement. Thus it was never certain that Simón Bolívar would emerge as the dominant independence leader of Venezuela. Santiago Mariño, Manuel Piar, José Bermúdez, Rafael Urdaneta, and Antonio José Sucre—all had successfully engaged the Spanish on multiple occasions; Manuel Piar as we've seen, rallied strong support among people of color; and José Antonio Páez earned the loyalty of the llaneros who had previously supported the Spaniards. The movement also included intellectuals of the caliber of Juan German Roscio, Cristobal Mendoza, Simón Rodríguez, and Andrés Bello. Against this backdrop, Bolívar distinguished himself by his ability to balance his talents as a statesman with those of a battlefield commander able to adapt to ever-shifting conditions.

As importantly, building on the earlier work of Francisco Miranda and Andrés Bello, Bolívar evolved a vision of the independence struggle in Venezuela as part of a continental enterprise. This hemispheric vision set his campaign apart from those of other independence leaders limited by a provincial outlook or satisfied with holding regional power. Bolívar operated on a grander scale, envisioning the former Spanish colonies of Nueva Granada (Colombia, Ecuador, and Venezuela) as a new nation able to rebuff Spain and chart its own course.

Even this notion of the nation, however, was not sufficient for Bolívar. He envisioned a Gran Patria, incorporating all of Latin America, where all former Spanish colonies would establish unity of action to compete on a world stage still dominated by Europe and subsequently the United States. His manifesto at Cartagena (1812), his aforementioned letter from Jamaica (1815), his speeches to the Congress at Angostura (1819), and his proposal for a continental congress at Panama (1826) all reveal an evolving vision for Latin America. Rebuffed on numerous occasions in his native Venezuela, challenged by political forces in Colombia and defeated by the Spanish on the battlefield, he never lost sight of the overarching struggle to which he dedicated his life.

Scholars typically divide Bolívar's life into four stages: his youth from 1783 until 1808, his formative intellectual period from 1808 until 1819, his military triumphs from 1819 to 1825, and the period from 1826 until his death in 1830. One of five children, Simón Bolívar was born in Caracas on July 24, 1783 (some sources suggest he was born at a family estate in the state of Aragua). As a prosperous slave-owning cacao grower and mine owner, his father maintained familial and social ties with the leading families that dominated colonial Venezuela. In 1735, the crown rejected Bolívar's grandfather's appeal to acquire a formal title of nobility since he could not prove the ancestry of a paternal great-grandmother thought by some to be either an African slave or Indian woman in the service of the family.

Unlike Bolívar, not all of his family supported independence. His sister María Antonia remained a monarchist her entire life, protecting Spaniards in her home and even writing to Spanish authorities to substantiate her loyalty to the crown. A distinguished member of local society, at age fifty-seven she became embroiled in a controversial extramartial relationship with a twenty-two-year-old *pardo*. The affair became public when she accused him of theft. In his defense, he produced love letters she had written him, inciting the Caracas rumor mill.

Like other *criollo* youth of his generation, Bolívar enjoyed a life of relative privilege despite the fact that both his parents died early on. Surrounded by attendants and educated by private tutors, he traveled to Europe in 1799 to pursue his studies. While in Spain, the nineteen-year-old Bolívar married María Teresa Toro and both traveled back to Caracas in 1802. Within months of arriving in Venezuela, however, she contracted yellow fever and died. Distraught, Bolívar returned to Europe for a second time.

With Bolívar, myth and fact are at times indistinguishable. While in Europe he engaged with the intellectual currents of the Enlightenment as well as British political theorists. The French Revolution and the independence movement in the United States also shaped his views of independence in Venezuela and Spanish America. In 1805, at Monte Sacro (Rome), while still only twenty-two, he dedicated his life to the cause of independence, proclaiming before his tutor Simón Rodríguez that he would not rest until Spain had been ousted from Venezuela. In 1806, he briefly stopped in New York and Philadelphia en route to Venezuela, where he joined the growing independence movement, emerging as the predominant leader of Venezuela, Colombia, Ecuador, Peru, and Bolivia, which bears his name.

Figure 1 A statue of Simon Bolívar, located in the Plaza Bolívar in the city center of Caracas. El Libertador is omnipresent in Venezuela.

How is Bolívar remembered today?

The study of Simón Bolívar has become a national obsession in Venezuela, where authors have written thousands of pages to trace his triumphs and tragedies. These books narrate his purported genealogy, his childhood, his voyages to Europe, the impact of his wife's early death, his contradictory views on post-independence society, his battlefield exploits, his continent-wide vision for Latin America, his romance with the Ecuadorean Manuela Saenz, his conflicts with independence figures in Venezuela and Colombia, and his death at forty-seven from tuberculosis.

"The Liberator" is everywhere in Venezuela (Figure 1). Every town has a Bolívar plaza, school, or monument, his presence serving to obscure other independence leaders.

Interestingly, Bolívar was denied such recognition in life; it was only after his death that he was elevated to the status of national hero. Since the latter part of the nineteenth century, political elites have exalted the image of Bolívar as the "father of the nation," a symbol that could serve to unify an otherwise fragmented country. The skillful manipulation of his legacy is evident throughout the twentieth century, as those in power have paid homage to him, while at times pursing policies that ran counter to his more progressive ideals.

Despite his overwhelming preeminence, Bolívar's legacy continues to generate controversy in Venezuela. Scion of a wealthy *criollo* family, he often held contradictory views on important political and social matters, including forms of governance and race. For most of the twentieth century, political elites and intellectuals dominated the national discourse over his ideals and minimized differences, fashioning a largely ceremonial "father of the nation."

However, there also existed a popular view of Bolívar, one embraced by progressive social movements and the left, in which his vision of Latin American integration, social issues, and education (to name a few topics) remained largely unfulfilled promises. Bolívar's concerns over the growing power of the United States bolstered his credentials as an anti-imperialist. In a letter to a British representative in Colombia, he cautioned that the United States "appeared destined to plague Latin America with misery in the name of liberty."

Thus two distinct views of Bolívar coexisted in Venezuela. The tension over these contrasting views appears in singer and songwriter Alí Primera's "Canción Bolívariana" which consists of a conversation between a young boy who tells Bolívar "the people have been deceived into thinking that the high bourgeoisie take flowers to the national pantheon every year on the anniversary of your death." Bolívar responds "Then what do they go for young compatriot?" The boy responds, "To make sure you are dead, very dead."

Bolívar's views remain the source of public discussions concerning the past and present course of Venezuelan politics and society. His contradictory views on democracy, race, international relations, social conditions, and public policy have bolstered a variety of positions taken by governments over the years. Efforts by the Chávez governments and social movements to ground their policies in Bolívar's legacy have led those opposing their reforms, including some academics, to deemphasize Bolívar's role in Venezuela. These actions would have been unthinkable throughout most of the twentieth century when Bolívar's legacy served as a central component of Venezuelan identity.

The schism about how to reinterpret the significance of the past and its heroes became evident with the opening of Bolívar's casket on July 16, 2010, which unleashed a vociferous yet predictable outcry in Venezuela. The mainstream media ridiculed the event, and conservative forces in Venezuela condemned it for purportedly desecrating Bolívar's remains. In the past, however, other politicians had opened Bolívar's casket as well. In fact, in 1947 the National Assembly publicly debated the authenticity of his remains and consulted with other "Bolívarian" nations, establishing a commission to make sure Bolívar's skeletal remains rested in the national pantheon. For many other Venezuelans, the opening of the casket, publicly televised, became a profoundly emotional moment, representing the first time that most Venezuelans had seen the purported remains of *El Liberator*. In contemporary Venezuela, Bolívar's legacy remains as contested as it was during the final chapter of his life when, prohibited from entering Venezuela, he lived in exile in Colombia, where he died on December 17, 1830.

What happened in Venezuelan politics and society after Bolívar?

Bolívar's dream of a unified Gran Colombia clashed with the personal ambitions and regional interests of political forces in the countries he had helped liberate. Although many in these countries recognized the importance of unified action to defeat the Spanish, they refused to cede power to a central authority once they achieved independence. Gradually, leaders in Venezuela, Colombia, Ecuador, and Peru began to chart their own course, and Bolívar's grand dream perished.

The wars of independence left Venezuela devastated with thousands dead and the economy in ruins. Some white elites fled the country and resettled elsewhere in the Caribbean, just as their counterparts in Haiti had done during the independence struggle. The war had a number of unintended consequences: the mobilization required to recruit soldiers by both sides forced people out of their isolated regions and exposed them to other Venezuelans of different races, social strata, and traditions. Such mobilization also swelled the number of men under arms in the service of *caudillos*—regional military leaders such as José Antonio Páez, Santiago Mariño, José Tadeo Monagas and others—who sought to translate their battlefield exploits into political power in the newly independent republic. At the very least, these figures sought recognition for their exploits and the resources to assure their economic status.

On the surface, the history of nineteenth-century Venezuela, much like its Latin America neighbors, appears as a legacy of *caudillos* placing personal interests above national priorities. Those unfamiliar with the history of the region have often resorted to explaining them with simplistic political analysis and racial stereotypes. They characterize these figures as petty dictators, the early equivalent of military strongmen that dominated the region in the twentieth century. Throughout the Americas, including the United States, the nineteenth century was a period of aggression against indigenous populations and devastating civil wars fought over competing national visions.

For former Spanish colonies, especially those with relatively weak elites, little or no consensus existed on what constituted a national project or even national interests. That is not to suggest that in Venezuela the *criollos* did not share a political vision or a class orientation. Though they retained influence and constituted an important force in their own local or regional context, the *criollo* elite lacked the power to impose a national consensus on the varied populations that inhabited regions as diverse as the Andes, the *llanos*, the coastal valleys, and the eastern hinterland. Moreover, they confronted opposition from sectors who had benefitted from the colonial order: from a Catholic Church unwilling to relinquish power, from foreign powers seeking economic concessions, and especially from laboring classes and people of color who often did not see any benefit in the new economic order and in some cases had alternative visions of the country. The absence of a hegemonic political or economic project and a dominant class able to exert control heightened the influence of independence era military leaders and regional *caudillos*, elevating them as arbiters of national politics.

Those in power throughout the nineteenth century also sought to alter social and racial conditions by promoting European immigration to Venezuela. Likewise, with little or no alternative, colonial era economic relations, in many cases dependent on a single crop (mono-export economies), deepened after independence. This made the newly independent republics vulnerable to meddling by foreign powers that exploited terms of trade, used credit as a means to exact concessions, and demanded protection for their investments in the country. Thus rather than simply an account of personal ambitions or chaotic conditions, much of the nineteenth century represents the incomplete character of the independence process, where full political independence was hampered by the lack of economic sovereignty, a condition that sometimes stimulated diverse internal interests to compete to impose their vision of the nation.

Why did José Antonio Páez emerge as the central figure after independence?

José Antonio Páez, the leader of the plainsmen whose tactics at the battle of Carabobo in 1821 turned the tide against the

Spanish, emerged as the leading political figure from 1830 until 1848. In May 1830, a new constitutional congress began to structure politics in the post-independence period. For Páez to consolidate his power, he had to weaken Bolívar's influence as well as that of other *caudillos* who still expressed rhetorical support for the Liberator and his ideals of the Gran Colombia. Some delegates to the congress even tried to condition bilateral relations with Bogota on Bolívar's expulsion from Colombia while pardoning several officers who had plotted his death. Seeking to limit Bolívar's influence, the delegates supported a limited form of federalism, one that reconciled the autonomy of the provinces with the central authority of the executive. The provinces continued to distrust Caracas' influence over national affairs. Moreover, the new political arrangement did little to reduce the power of regional elites. Páez served as the guarantor of the new political arrangement, using his personal prestige to assuage the opposition.

The constitution, however, did curtail the power of the Catholic Church, limiting its ability to collect tithes, and remained silent on the existence of a national religion. Many of Venezuela's political and intellectual leaders—including Miranda, Bolívar, Roscio, Páez, Monagas, and many others—belonged to the Masonic order and as Masons they shared a distrust of the Church. In this, Venezuela's political elites differed from other postcolonial nations in Latin America that deferred to the Church. This does not imply an anti-Catholic inclination among elites, but rather the desire to avoid economic competition from the Church and to establish the independence of the state.

The congress also abolished special privileges for the military (*fueros*), subjecting them to civilian justice. Delegates restricted the presidency to a single four-year term. They adopted male suffrage for those over twenty-one, literate, and who owned property; they would select the delegates who in turn would elect the president. To appease slaveowning agricultural interests, delegates restricted efforts begun in 1821 to institute manumission (freedom for those born after a certain date), thereby ensuring the continuation of slavery. In effect the 1830 congress reinstated colonial era privileges for the landowning *criollo* class and commercial elites who feared losing power in the aftermath of independence. Although the formal exclusionary language that had heavily favored the white elites during the colonial regime was left out, nothing adopted in the 1830 constitution radically altered the existing social or racial hierarchy. Conditions for the rural poor, many surviving as indebted peons, tied them to a cycle of debt that proved indistinguishable from slavery. Most could not change domicile without permission from local authorities; their "benefactor" maintained the right to sell their debt to others as property. In short the wars of independence may have resulted in a rupture with Spain, but they did not produce a social revolution that altered preexisting class relations or redistributed wealth. As expected, Páez assumed the presidency of the newly independent Republic of Venezuela in 1831, which was presided over by conservatives known as *"godos"* who sought to reestablish their control in the wake of the independence era's social ferment.

Opposition to the constitution was immediate, and erupted among multiple sectors, including Afro-Venezuelans, for whom independence remained an unfulfilled promise; the Catholic hierarchy; and the independence leaders. Racial divisions that plagued the independence process reemerged in May 1831 when a group of mostly Afro-Venezuelans stormed the Caracas jail and attacked *criollos*, sacking their property and threatening to turn Venezuela, in the words of one foreign visitor, into a "second Haiti." As the Spanish authorities had done previously when they faced rebellions led by people of color, the government quickly repressed the movement and executed its leaders. The Páez government had an easier time dealing with clerics who refused to proclaim loyalty to the new constitution, simply expelling them from the country.

The military leaders and the troops loyal only to them proved to be a more challenging threat. The generals who had prosecuted the wars of independence were unwilling to relinquish their power without first obtaining concessions. For instance, in eastern Venezuela, José Tadeo Monagas refused to recognize the new constitution and defended Bolívar's legacy largely as a way of asserting his own prerogatives. As he did on multiple occasions, Páez personally assumed charge of the negotiations with the rebels, using his personal prestige to avert open conflict and maintain national unity. Nevertheless, rebellions by independence era military officers, as well as racially inspired conflicts, plagued Venezuela throughout the Páez presidency.

Why couldn't elites forge a consensus?

As Páez's term ended and a new election was held, political factions, composed mostly of ex-military leaders, landed elites, and commercial sectors disputed the results. Nonetheless, the old oligarchy imposed their candidate, José María Vargas, who assumed the presidency in 1835. Páez turned over power to Vargas and retired to manage his estates.

The Venezuelan economy continued to depend on colonial era agricultural products such as coffee and cacao for exports, along with dyes and hides. Lacking capital, merchant houses and their foreign representatives in Caracas and Maracaibo exercised control by providing access to credit. Many landowners unable to complete payment on a predetermined schedule lost their property.

By the 1830s, coffee surpassed other exports, growing threefold during the period dominated by Páez. Thus besides a personal quest for influence, conflict between regional leaders belied a struggle by local elites to dispute power and to control the emerging agro-export economy that linked Venezuela to the imperatives of the world economy. None of the rebellions led by former independence leaders during this period proposed an alternative vision of the nation, one that might have involved a restructuring of social and racial relations or economic exchange with the outside world. These former leaders, however, had little trouble recruiting unemployed men with hopes of collecting bounty if their rebellion proved successful.

Within months of assuming office, Vargas confronted an open rebellion by self-proclaimed reformers—largely former independence military leaders including Mariño, Monagas, and several others—who exiled him from the country. Páez marched from the plains and reestablished the Vargas government. To preserve the delicate balance of power he once again pardoned the rebels, who took refuge in eastern Venezuela under the protection of Monagas.

Páez's handling of the rebellion contributed to his standing as the principal mediator of Venezuelan politics in the post-independence period, where institutions remained frail and *caudillo* politics carried the day. Nonetheless, Vargas did not last, and a few months after returning to power he resigned, leaving Páez to mediate once again between political factions. After several interim presidents, Páez returned to the presidency in 1839, although he often spent time on his estates and left the government in hands of his vice presidents.

During the Páez presidency, bands of guerrillas, some formed along racial lines, regularly raided haciendas and preyed on travelers and merchants. Although he proved adept at handling differences between rival *caudillos* and the Caracas power elite, Páez had a more difficult time controlling the Venezuelan countryside. By 1836, the congress approved public hangings for guerrilla leaders and 150 lashings—nearly a death sentence—for individuals involved in property related crimes.

What was the importance of the Liberal Party?

Even as Páez appeared to consolidate power, political forces organized to challenge his rule. An eclectic mix of old elites, landowners, and political interests formed Venezuela's first official party in 1840, the *Partido Liberal* (Liberal Party—endorsing free trade but not progressive social policy) and by 1842 began to publish the *El Venezolano* (The *Venezuelan)* as their mouthpiece. Claiming opposition to the economic policies of the Páez regime, the privilege it afforded foreign economic interests, and the reviled 1834 law of contracts used to foreclose on property, liberals openly criticized the government. Except for the desire to assume power, programmatically little separated the new Liberal Party from its conservative opponents. In fact, Antonio Leocadio Guzmán, one of the new party's principal spokespersons, stated that "if our opponents had declared in favor of federalism we would have declared in favor of centralism."

As previously mentioned, after independence Venezuela's economy became increasingly dependent on coffee exports, subjecting the country to the vicissitudes of the international market. During the 1830s the country benefited from increased prices in agricultural commodities. However, during the 1840s those declined, sending reverberations throughout the economy and affecting commercial interests, property owners, and the rural poor. The absence of independent sources of credit to mitigate the crisis worsened conditions.

As was the case throughout Latin America, most Venezuelan elites functioned as intermediaries in the international market for agricultural commodities. Yet although they controlled huge tracts of land and with the support of the state could manipulate access to labor, they remained a weak social class with little actual capital. The relative feebleness of Venezuela's elite classes increased their reliance on the state and influenced policy decisions throughout the nineteenth century. To compensate, the country increasingly became indebted to English commercial interests, a policy that allowed the British to exercise greater influence in the country. As the population neared 1.2 million, efforts by the government to attract European immigrants became a source of debate. A handful of Germans established a still-famous agricultural colony in 1841, although it bore little fruit: the total number of immigrants entering the port at La Guaira between 1832 and 1845 barely exceeded sixteen thousand.

As the price of exports collapsed, imports continued to increase and Venezuela's debt with England became a political matter. While offering little in the way of significant change, the liberals led by Guzmán openly manipulated popular discontent against the government to gain political ground on the conservatives. In 1843, outside of Caracas in the Tuy Valley, landowners burned the image of Páez and copies of the hated 1834 law of contracts. During 1846, a popular insurrection led by Francisco Rangel and Ezequiel Zamora demanded communal lands and popular elections. These rebellions exemplified the growing discontent with the conservative ruling elite and expressed popular sentiments in favor of land distribution, an end to slavery, and increased political participation. Although the government succeeded in quashing the rebellions, the social demands persisted.

Were the Federal Wars of 1858–1863 inevitable?

Having weathered several crises during the early 1840s, Páez and the conservatives prepared to nominate Rafael Urdaneta, an independence hero from the western state of Zulia, for president in 1846. His premature death left the conservatives without a candidate; hoping to prevent further revolts and strike a conciliatory note, Páez supported the candidacy of a previous rival José Tadeo Monagas, a *caudillo* from eastern Venezuela. Easily elected, once in office Monagas (1847–1851) allied with the liberals and commuted death sentences against Loecadio Guzmán and rebels such as Zamora, earning the enmity of the conservatives in Congress, who tried to remove him from power. Monagas eventually dissolved Congress, only to later reconstitute it under his control. Hoping to repeat events of 1835, Páez organized an army. Conditions had changed, however, and the old general had become estranged from the forces he previously commanded. After being defeated at the battle of Los Araguatos in 1848 he sought asylum in Colombia. Subsequently captured in 1849 and paraded through streets in irons, after a brief incarceration he was exiled by the government to the United States. Páez continued to be involved in Venezuela politics, returning in 1858 and briefly holding power in 1861, before returning to New York where he died in 1873.

Though José Tadeo Monagas and the liberals altered the unpopular 1834 law of contracts and ended the death penalty for political crimes, they lacked an alternative vision of the nation. Instead, Monagas took measures to protect landed economic interests during periods of crisis without altering Venezuela's reliance on agricultural commodities.

In addition to fluctuations in coffee prices, Venezuela continued to suffer from lack of infrastructure and access to credit and marketing at a time when other countries in the region had begun to compete on the world market. Divisions among landed interests also became evident, as the old oligarchy with roots in the colonial period competed for resources with the military rebels and independence figures who had acquired land under the *Ley de Repartos* (Law of Distribution) in the past thirty years. Facing new elections and intent on preserving power, Monagas supported his brother José Gregorio (1851–1855), who assumed the presidency, generating protests among both liberals and conservatives.

Rebellions dogged Gregorio's presidency. Facing conservative willingness to mobilize slaves, in 1854 Monagas took a dramatic step and abolished slavery, promising full compensation to former owners. Emancipation did little to improve conditions for thousands of former slaves, however—most continued to toil on rural estates under deplorable conditions. In an effort to perpetuate the Monagas dynasty, José Tadeo once again assumed the presidency in 1855, aggravating political conditions, and within a short time opposition forces ousted him from office.

At one level, the Federal Wars reflected the inconclusive nature of the independence process that had left colonial society largely intact. In fact, some scholars argue that with independence, landed interests and the commercial class expanded their control over economic activity at the expense of smaller producers and those outside the formal economy. In this sense, the Federal Wars essentially represented dissonant elite political positions that sought to defend their interests and control politics, and thus the export economy.

In another sense, however, the era of the Federal Wars embodied unresolved social, class, and even racial cleavages evident in Venezuelan society since before independence. For the great majority of Venezuelans policies adopted by the old conservative oligarchy or their new liberal coun terparts had done little to improve their plight. Recently freed slaves, the landless, people of color, and the urban poor filled the ranks of the guerrilla bands that at various times took control of the countryside. The more radical pronouncements for racial and social equality and land distribution undoubtedly motivated many among these sectors to join the liberal cause. Many others, however, joined the rebel armies and guerrilla bands, inspired more by regional loyalties and economic imperatives than by politics or ideology. Facing this general mobilization and fearing the outcome of the conflict, which was effectively Venezuela's Civil War, in 1861 a group of conservative landowners actually requested British intervention.

The Federal Wars entered a new phase when liberals such as Zamora, Leocadio Guzman, and Juan Crisóstomo Falcón secretly prepared a rebellion in 1859. Falcón served as the titular head of the movement, but Zamora became its leading figure and most popular leader. A menacing war, proclaiming "Oligarcas Temblad" ("Oligarchs Tremble"), reminded many elites of the earlier "War to the Death" during wars of independence. Although guerrilla skirmishes flared with frequency, the decisive battle of the period occurred at Santa Ines in 1859;

under Zamora's leadership, the insurgent army set ablaze the dry plain's brush, wiping out the government's troops.

Zamora's appeal among the poor increased and he emerged as the undisputed leader of the movement. Differences emerged with Falcón over taking Caracas, the capital. Away from the battlefield, a bullet struck Zamora, mortally wounding him. Some suspect his liberal allies, who distrusted radical pronouncements in favor of equality, might have ordered him killed. One conservative writer of the period described the gunshot that killed Zamora as the "fortunate bullet."

Hated by the conservatives and never fully trusted by liberals, Zamora found few positive treatments by Venezuelan historians until he was embraced in the 20th century by social movements and subsequently the Chávez government, who elevated him to the status of a martyr who championed land reform and social equality. This interpretation finds inspiration in the victory at Santa Inés, and insists that Zamora's actions, and those of other social reformers, should motivate a reassessment of nineteenth-century history long neglected by traditional scholars.

After Zamora's death the war continued, with Páez and Monagas reappearing on the political stage. In the end Falcón emerged victorious in 1863, heading a new coalition that included Antonio Guzmán Blanco (son of Leocadio Guzmán). A peace treaty signed in 1863 put a formal end to the Federal Wars, one of the bloodiest episodes in the country's history, leaving over 100,000 dead, decimating the economy, and swelling the foreign debt.

How did post-Federal War Venezuela evolve?

The Federal Wars may have ended but political and social conflict continued. A series of presidents. including Falcón and Monagas, briefly assumed power before Antonio Guzmán Blanco led a revolt in 1870 and assumed leadership of the Liberal Party. Similar to other liberals of this era in Latin

America, Guzmán Blanco (three terms between 1870 and 1887), who preferred the title of the "Illustrious American," promoted the construction of an independent state apparatus that could contain violence, promote a modern bureaucracy, and revitalize the economy in order to ensure export-based revenue. In return for recognizing the central authority of the federal government, local elites preserved a degree of autonomy to oversee local matters. A revival of coffee exports, in part due to expanded production in the Venezuelan Andes, increased state revenues, permitting Guzmán Blanco to appease political opponents and expand the state bureaucracy. Despite often employing a nationalist rhetoric, the government favored relations with foreign investors, protecting their assets and granting concessions to exploit Venezuela's resources.

Under Guzmán Blanco, the contours of the modern state took shape, placing limits on the power of the church while advancing secular public education, a national civil registry, a network of roads, and the expansion of the armed forces. To accentuate the importance of the central government and the growing bureaucracy, Caracas, with a population nearing 50,000 residents, underwent a dramatic facelift that increased its preeminence over the other regions. Influenced by the prevailing positivist ideals of the era, the Guzmán Blanco government followed the lead of several other Latin American nations and promoted foreign immigration, managing to attract several thousand immigrants, mostly Canary Islanders who went on to assume an important role in agriculture and commerce.

Despite these liberal reforms, conditions for the common Venezuelan did not improve substantially. Poverty and tropical diseases limited life expectancy, while the power of the proprietor classes remained unchallenged. The liberal reforms and the modernization of the state pursued by the Guzmán Blanco government represented a concerted effort by elites to vanquish obstacles, including the Church or the *caudillos*, that prevented them from exercising power over the state and the economy. Directly or indirectly, Guzmán Blanco himself amassed significant personal wealth by extracting funds from the national treasury and deriving profit from contracts signed with foreign interests. He controlled Venezuela for eighteen years, often relinquishing power to travel to Europe as plenipotentiary minister of Venezuela and eventually retiring to Paris, where he died in 1899.

The general contours of changes promoted by Guzmán Blanco endured, though still not fully institutionalized; they continued to depend on the political climate and the individual in power. Coffee remained the leading export, generating a dangerous dependence on a single agro-export product. An increase in production and the price of coffee during the early 1890s concealed the vulnerability of the Venezuelan economy. In reality, except for coffee and a few other export crops, Venezuelan agriculture had evolved little since the colonial period. Only a handful of estates actually produced for local markets, and most farming reflected subsistence agriculture.

The political climate remained turbulent as several presidents faltered or found themselves removed from office before Joaquín Crespo (1892–1898) emerged as the dominant political figure of the last decade of the nineteenth century. Although the country adopted universal male suffrage for anyone over eighteen in 1893, political chicanery still determined the outcome. In fact, Crespo died in battle in 1898, attempting to put down a rebellion against his chosen successor for the presidency.

Who was Cipriano Castro and how did the Andeans come to dominate Venezuela?

In 1898, the price of coffee again plummeted, exposing the vulnerability of dependence on a single crop. Taking advantage of the unstable political and economic climate, Cipriano Castro, who hailed from the Andes mountain region, raised an army and marched on Caracas, launching a self-proclaimed Liberal Restoration. The rise of Castro, who became president in

1899, marks the ascendancy of a succession of Andean rulers in Venezuela, a phenomenon that lasted over forty-five years. Rather than some aberration in Venezuelan history, the rise to power of the Andinos (people from Táchira, Mérida, and Trujillo) represented a continuation of the liberal nation-building agenda evident throughout the nineteenth century.

Castro's ascendancy is rooted in the legacy of conflict that Venezuela experienced beginning in the middle of the nineteenth century. Castro's birth state of Táchira bordered Colombia, and like many Andinos he experienced first-hand the nuances of living in a border region where family, commerce, and tradition linked people on both sides of the international boundary. San Cristóbal, the capital of Táchira, served as a point of encounter and transit connecting the Andes, the *llanos*, Maracaibo, and Colombia. Trade in coffee drove the economy of western Venezuela and the adjacent Colombian region of Norte Santander. The state had also experienced a dramatic population increase, more than doubling in size in less than two decades. Unlike the traditional landed oligarchy that monopolized property elsewhere in Venezuela, the Andes experienced multiple forms of land ownership: medium and small producers, sharecroppers, and a class of agricultural wage laborers. These forms of production and labor practice stamped the region, its politics, and its culture.

With the port city of Maracaibo as its central axis, the coffee trade included three Andean states—Táchira, Mérida, and Trujillo—and the piedmont region of Barinas and nearby Colombia. Fueled by capital, mostly in the forms of loans from commercial houses in Maracaibo (many controlled by Germans), and labor migrating from Barinas and Colombia, the coffee industry began to expand during the 1830s. An intricate network of overland routes, railroads, and waterways connected the Andean region to Maracaibo and then by sea to international markets. Isolated in western Venezuela, the region had also avoided the dislocation produced by repeated conflicts elsewhere in the country.

Castro attended seminary school and dabbled in liberal politics in Colombia before returning to work for a German-controlled trading house in his native state. Although described by some as illiterate, in actual fact at an early age he began to write for a weekly newspaper and exchanged ideas with leading intellectuals. His association with liberal causes in Colombia, where he spent several years in exile, became evident throughout his later administration in repeated clashes and in the eventual rupture in relations with the conservative governments in Bogota. Concerned by the expansion of US power in the Caribbean, particularly in the aftermath of the war in Cuba in 1898, and by European actions against his own country, Castro adopted a nationalist posture in dealing with foreign economic and political interests.

During Castro's formative years, he took part in several revolts that supported autonomy for Táchira, where he eventually assumed the governorship and subsequently served as federal deputy to the national congress. In 1899, together with his *compadre* Juan Vicente Gómez and a handful of Andean supporters, he marched on Caracas. After several battles, he assumed power over a country ravaged by civil wars, with an unstable economy and owing millions to foreign powers. Castro's forces, mostly *campesinos* (rural laborers), initially confounded the people of Caracas who came out to see the *gochos* (Andeans) that talked, looked, and dressed differently from the locals. Once in office, Castro and his allies successfully defeated a succession of conservative-supported rebellions, dismantling the power of regional political chiefdoms and eliminating them as a decisive factor in national politics. The successful campaigns spearheaded in most cases by Juan Vicente Gómez increased the power and prestige of Castro's then-principal ally and future nemesis.

Employing the rhetoric of economic nationalism, Castro also expanded the role of a state-sponsored national military and promoted the growth of an administrative bureaucratic class begun under Guzmán Blanco. Castro also negotiated the first asphalt and contracts for oil exploration in Venezuela, initiating a process that would eventually transform the country. The most important concessions the government made occurred in 1907, when they granted over four million hectares in Zulia, near Lake Maracaibo, that were eventually acquired by British and Dutch interests who monopolized most production sites in the region. Even though he oversaw these first concessions, Castro's wariness toward foreign powers and the promotion of economic nationalism would distinguish him from the subsequent openly conciliatory policy adopted by his successor, Juan Vicente Gómez.

Why did European powers blockade Venezuela in 1902?

On December 7, 1902, the Venezuelan government received an ultimatum from the British and German governments to pay a series of purported claims or face a naval blockade of its ports. After consulting with the United States, the European powers, including Italy, demanded repayment of loans made to the government that included, among others, funds for the construction of a railroad and losses suffered by their citizens during Venezuela's recurring civil wars. On December 11, British and German ships began the blockade, stationing ships at the country's principal ports, including Maracaibo, Puerto Cabello, and La Guaira, where they seized several Venezuelan naval vessels. They also landed troops to withdraw diplomats, and in Puerto Cabello they bombarded the Venezuelan fort that guarded the entrance to the port.

The blockade occurred on the heels of another international humiliation for Venezuela. In October 1899, an international tribunal in Paris granted London control over disputed territory in the neighboring British colony of Guyana, angering Venezuelans and increasing tensions with European powers. Venezuela had initially hoped to submit this dispute to mediation by a body consisting of Latin American nations. Instead, an international body dominated by the United States and Britain, with no Venezuelan delegate, adjudicated the issue. Former US President Benjamin Harrison represented Venezuela; however, needless to say, the country's prospects of prevailing in a tribunal dominated by foreign powers appeared slim. In their unanimous decision, offered without supporting rationale, the United States, British, and Russian judges ruled against Venezuela. In the parlance of the period, the tribunal "allowed" Venezuela to retain the Orinoco river delta in return for accepting the decision that sustained British claims to over ninety percent of the territory. Venezuela probably received control of the Orinoco River delta because the United States did not want Britain to control access to the second most important waterway in South America.

Although commercial oil production had not fully materialized, Venezuela nonetheless retained geopolitical importance as a gateway to the Caribbean and a rich source of natural commodities. Even before the formal blockade, tensions with the Europeans increased. Germans and British represented the principal foreign interests operating in Venezuela, and German merchants dominated the trade in coffee through the port of Maracaibo. German reconnaissance of the coast of Venezuela had also intensified. Rumors circulated that Germany sought a coaling station on a nearby island and on several occasions foreign seamen clashed with Venezuelan authorities while their ships were in port.

Accustomed to dealing with more accommodating political leaders in the region, the Europeans and the United States disliked Castro's firm stance. Depictions of Castro in United States' diplomatic cables and in the foreign press accentuated his dark skin and described him as an impertinent child, possessing a Napoleonic complex, or worse depicted him as a "megalomaniacal tropical dictator" incapable of governing his country. Criticism of Castro constantly brought up his goal to reconstitute the Gran Colombia, a not-so-subtle criticism of Simón Bolívar and Latin American unity in general. Traditional historiography, from both the left and the right, tends to reproduce these characterizations. Castro's place in history has been reevaluated by some contemporary scholars, and the Chávez government stressed his nationalist economic policies and distrust of imperial powers. At the time, the racially inspired slanders and other affronts did not keep Venezuela's plight from drawing sympathy from Argentina, Peru, and other Latin American countries concerned about the precedent implicit in the ability of foreign powers to invade a country in order to collect claims made by its citizens.

Facing the blockade shortly after assuming power and confronting a drop in the price of coffee as well as several internal rebellions, the Castro government sought to rally nationalist sentiments. Castro proclaimed the need to uphold "National Unity" in the face of international aggression, declaring in a speech "Venezuelans, the boot of the insolent foreigner has profaned the sacred soil of our country." In Caracas, several thousand people volunteered to join the military while others burned foreign flags and lashed out at British and German citizens and their interests. Castro also promoted restraint: according to the *Times*, he declared that "however great our indignation, we must behave as a cultured and civilized people, especially when the most powerful nations of Europe are behaving like real savages."

Beyond the naval blockade, European interests previously had lent financial support to Manuel Matos, a former banker who led a "Liberating Revolution" against the government. With financing from British, French, and German interests, Matos obtained a ship and weapons and provided them to local *caudillos* seeking to get rid of Castro. They clashed with government forces commanded by Castro at the battle of La Victoria that ended after a month in Matos's defeat and hundreds of casualties.

Despite the use of nationalist rhetoric, in the end Castro accepted a proposal made by Caracas's leading merchants to have United States envoy Herbert Bowen mediate the crisis. Castro had proposed setting aside thirty percent of income from the customs houses at Puerto Cabello and La Guaira to pay the foreign debt. Although the United States had initially accepted the British and German blockade it feared losing control in the region. At the behest of Venezuela, it mediated a largely symbolic solution between the parties that resembled Castro's original proposal.

In the aftermath of the experiences with Venezuela, the Theodore Roosevelt administration issued its famous corollary to the Monroe Doctrine in 1904 asserting the United States government's rights to police the region, manage finances, and exclude the Europeans. Despite the controversy, the incident established Venezuela's presence in the region, and after the crisis, Castro sent representatives to England to improve Venezuela's image in Europe.

What were social and racial conditions like on the eve of the twentieth century?

The majority of Venezuelans had experienced little significant improvement in their lives since gaining independence from Spain at the beginning of the nineteenth century. Coffee continued to dominate agricultural exports and increase the value of land in productive areas, displacing the production of traditional subsistence crops. Despite extensive territory, throughout much of the nineteenth century the country's arable land under actual cultivation remained exceedingly small, mainly concentrated in pockets in the Andes and the central valleys of Venezuela. With few roads in operation, access to the Caribbean provided the most efficient form of transportation for areas in proximity to the coast.

Cities linked to the coffee export economy such as Carúpano in the east, San Cristobal in the west, the port of Maracaibo, and the capital, Caracas, acquired the outward veneer of progress, including electrical lighting, paved streets and sidewalks, aqueducts, police services, horse-drawn urban trains, central markets, municipal theaters, and even bull rings. Cities' leaders undertook efforts to modernize the urban environment, adopting health and uniform building codes, imposing vagrancy laws, limiting possession of animals, prohibiting possession of weapons, restricting gambling and social celebrations, and confining prostitution to certain areas. For segments of the population, stores offering finished products such as textiles, general consumer goods, and foodstuffs also introduced new patterns of consumption. A series of interlocking networks sustained the cities, connecting the international export economy with the rural countryside from where they derived their wealth. Beyond the economic level, the networks also operated on a social one, linking local elites with foreigners who served as intermediaries for the export of coffee.

Yet such efforts did not reach all sectors of the population. As with the rest of Venezuela, the cities remained socially stratified. In the shadow of the modern urban center, the poor who serviced the labor needs of the city lived in substandard housing, with limited access to water or other necessities. For the well-off, cities were viewed as islands of civilization surrounded by a backward countryside where the majority of the population resided. Urban elites thus appropriated the role of agents of civilization confronting a superstitious and at times hostile rural population that consisted of mostly people of color or mixed-race individuals. As they had in the early part of the century, pronounced racial and social differences continued to determine interaction between people of diverse ethnic groups.

In the countryside, most people eked out an existence by selling their labor, sharecropping, and engaging in various forms of subsistence agriculture on individual plots known as *conucos*, an Arawak term employed throughout the Caribbean. They lived in residences made from *bahareque* (a local form of adobe), thatched palm roofs, and dirt floors. They mostly cooked on wood stoves, the smoke from which penetrated everything in the residence. Many people slept on *hamacas* (hammocks) that hung from the walls. The diet of the average person consisted of grains, tubers, and only occasionally meat. Regional variations included greater access to wheat and potato in the Andes, local tubers and squashes in the east, and beef in the *llanos*. Most attire consisted of cheap white cloth, and shoes consisted of *alpargatas*, leather soles covered in cloth or tied with rope (resembling Mexican *huaraches*). Gender differences influenced recreation: men attended cockfights, *coleadas de toros* (steer wrestling), horseracing, and gambling; women organized town-sponsored festivities, dances, social celebrations, and religious activities.

Education was largely nonexistent in the countryside, which meant that most people were illiterate. At the turn of the nineteenth century, upwards of eighty-five percent of the country could not read. Besides the recurrent patterns of conflict evident throughout the nineteenth century, the tropical countryside also proved unhealthy. Insects, poisonous snakes, as well as outbreaks of cholera and yellow fever combined to reduce life expectancy. By 1900, Venezuela had a population of nearly 2.5 million people, the great majority—over eighty percent—residing in rural areas. Caracas, the capital, had a population of close to 100,000. Venezuela had one of the lowest levels of population density in Latin America, with five inhabitants per square mile, and most areas remained self-contained, isolated territories with no viable communication routes.

Patterns set in motion during the colonial era continued to influence where people lived. The valleys of the north coastal mountain range—areas that had produced cacao, sugar and other crops—evidenced the greatest concentration of people: about sixty percent of the population inhabited approximately twenty percent of the national territory. Other pockets of population density included the eastern coastal region between Carupano and Cumana and the Andean states connected to the lake and port of Maracaibo. Efforts by the authorities to impose vagrancy laws, enforce debt collection, and employ other repressive measures did little to relocate the population to areas that purportedly required laborers.

The abolition of slavery in 1854 did not materially improve the lives of former slaves. Most remained on estates where they still faced strict labor controls. The absence of formal segregation laws did not mean that racial prejudice ceased to be a factor in the interaction between social groups. This matter remains a subject of some controversy in Venezuela, where the prevailing national narrative promotes the view that racism lost ground in the latter decades of the nineteenth century. While acknowledging the historic role of discrimination and segregation, and the popular resentment that existed against so-called *"gente de sangre azul"* (bluebloods), one renowned anthropologist argued that the Federal Wars produced a "democratization of relations between human groups . . . which was facilitated by the elimination of the prejudices that previously stamped these relations."[2]

This argument, however, fails to acknowledge that the dominant social and racial aesthetic, the product of three hundred years of colonial rule, had been grafted onto the notions of social and economic class. Moreover, it fails to recognize that race in Venezuela was not simply a matter that differentiated white elites from a homogeneous group of people of color. In Venezuela, people of color, but especially *pardos*, embodied complex differences and stratifications influenced by class, education, social standing, and even phenotype that complicate broad generalizations concerning race and social standing.

The democratization argument also fails to recognize that, when in power, middle- and upper-class *pardos* (who by now occupied the most important public posts) replicated racial hierarchies in their social interactions with Indians, former slaves, and other people of color. The entry of these groups into new social circles did not undermine the prevailing dominant white aesthetic. On the contrary, to affirm their new standing, *pardos* replicated racial and social prejudice and subjected people of color to the same discrimination they themselves previously experienced.

Notes

1. Arlene Diaz, *Female Citizens, Patriarchs, and the Law in Caracas, Venezuela, 1786–1904* (Lincoln: The University of Nebraska Press, 2004).

2. Rodolfo Quintero, cited in Federico Brito Figueroa, *Ensayos de historia social venezolana* (Caracas: Universidad Central de Venezuela, 1960), p. 328.

Part Two

VENEZUELA IN THE TWENTIETH CENTURY

When was oil discovered?

Petroleum and natural gas seeps, produced by fissures in the earth, dot the landscape in various regions of eastern and western Venezuela. The indigenous people labeled these occurrences *menes*, and they used the viscous substance to weatherproof structures, light torches, or caulk their crafts. The Spanish conquistadores who arrived in the sixteenth century recorded its presence and sent samples to Spain, but found no practical uses for the oily substance.

In the middle of the nineteenth century, petroleum products, principally asphalt, began to acquire commercial value and the government granted several contracts for extraction, including some to foreigners. In 1878, a group of Venezuelans established the Petrolia Oil Company and began to extract oil in the Andean state of Táchira, near the Colombian border. At first, they excavated a natural seep and collected oil using buckets. Eventually, they established a small drilling operation and distillation facility that supplied the needs of the adjacent area.

In eastern Venezuela, by the 1880s the vast Guanoco pitch lake drew the attention of foreign investors interested in exporting asphalt to pave an ever-expanding network of roads in the United States. A dense tropical environment and diseases complicated operations, however. After several failed attempts, another US outfit, the New York and Bermudez Company, acquired the rights to the site and began production. The company employed several hundred Venezuelan and Trinidadian laborers who carved out blocks of tar weighing upwards of seventy pounds that eventually reached foreign markets by ship. The company also drilled several wells near the lake, but the viscosity of the oil made operations unfeasible.

Having openly supported opponents of Cipriano Castro, the Bermudez Company became embroiled in a dispute with the government that lead to the curtailment of its operations. Although it experienced a brief boom during World War I, operators eventually abandoned the site. Despite initial difficulties, the experiences at Guanoco and elsewhere served to highlight Venezuela as a potential rich deposit of oil and not just asphalt.

Recognizing the newfound and growing importance of oil for engines and industrial machinery, in 1907 several Venezuelan interests staked claims to extensive tracks of land near Lake Maracaibo and the western region of the country where oil seeps appeared naturally. Before long, British interests acquired these claims from Venezuelans, and several teams of foreign and Venezuelan geologists scoured the countryside exploring locations that could yield petroleum. Based largely on these reports, the British Caribbean Petroleum Company initiated drilling at Mene Grande in the western state of Zulia and by July 1914 the Zumaque N. 1 was producing about 150 barrels per day.

The wells at Mene Grande and the construction of a refinery at San Lorenzo near the lakeshore marked the formal entrance of Venezuela into the era of commercial oil production. Even as they continued to expand operations at the Mene Grande facility, Caribbean Petroleum and Venezuelan Oil Concessions (VOC), future subsidiaries of Shell Oil, began to drill near the shore of Lake Maracaibo, the largest body of fresh water in

South America. Between 1914 and 1920, Caribbean Petroleum and VOC successfully located deposits and drilled dozens of wells along the eastern shore of the lake. On December 14, 1922, at a site known as La Rosa, crews for the VOC felt the ground under their feet tremble. At fifteen hundred feet, drillers had perforated a vast underground deposit of oil that erupted with such ferocity that it spewed over one hundred thousand barrels a day. News of the discovery of La Rosa traveled over wire services, quickly reaching New York and London. For Venezuela, the well at La Rosa inaugurated the legendary *El Dorado* that had previously eluded the Spanish. Before long, dozens of foreign companies and hundreds of workers descended on Venezuela, initiating a process that would forever transform the country.

Already heavily invested in Mexico, United States interests proved unprepared for new developments in Venezuela. To compensate, US companies wooed government officials to ensure access to concessions. Eager to strike a balance between competing foreign interests and not wanting the British to monopolize the emerging industry, the Venezuelan government acceded to US requests. Surmising that shore deposits must extend underground into the actual lake, US companies staked out their claims. Companies such as Lago Petroleum and Gulf Oil built precarious wooden structures that allowed them to drill over the water, and made important discoveries that assured their presence in the country. Drilling along the lakeshore and over the water initiated the environmental degradation of the lake, a condition that continues unabated to this day. An uncharted jumble of rusted pipes and sunken platforms rests at the bottom of Lake Maracaibo. Eventually more than a hundred foreign companies and thousands of foreigners from the United States and elsewhere arrived in Venezuela, seeking to benefit from the oil bonanza.

The oil industry experienced dramatic periods of expansion and contraction during the decade of the 1920s and 1930s. Eventually three enterprises, Standard Oil Company

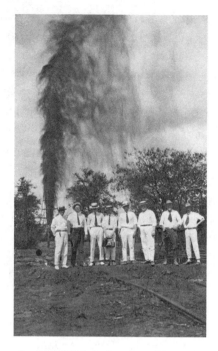

Figure 2 The Barroso II well. In 1922, the well established Venezuela as a leading producer of oil.

(later Creole Petroleum), Shell Oil and, to a lesser extent, Mene Grande (Gulf Oil) emerged as the dominant firms with established production sites and new residential quarters for its employees. By 1926 oil displaced coffee as the leading export and by 1928 Venezuela became the world's second-leading exporter of petroleum and the first by 1935 (Figure 2).

What impact did oil production have on Venezuelan society?

Initially, because of their isolation, production sites such as Lake Guanaco in eastern Venezuela and Mene Grande in the west had little impact on local society. For most Venezuelans, news of the discovery of oil spread slowly. The oil companies, eager to contract laborers, at first dealt with local landed interests or used labor contractors to recruit workers to staff drilling operations. As the industry moved beyond these remote sites and established a presence along the eastern Lake Maracaibo shore, the demand for labor increased dramatically.

Eager to benefit from higher wages, residents of the nearby states of Trujillo, Falcón, Lara, and the island of Margarita responded to the new labor needs and descended on the lakeshore communities. In addition to Venezuelans and US expatriates, Afro-West Indians and Chinese, mainly from the British-controlled islands of Trinidad and Granada, sought to take advantage of the oil bonanza. Racial and cultural tensions between these groups proved common and often government and company officials exacerbated conditions by favoring foreigners.

Existing settlements along the lakeshore such as Cabimas, Tía Juana, and Lagunillas proved incapable of incorporating the arrival of hundreds of new laborers. For most Venezuelan newcomers, living quarters consisted of exposed open-air thatched roof structures where dozens of workers took turns sleeping while others went off to work. The foreign crews—mostly tool pushers, machinist, drillers, and supervisors—slept in tents or improvised wooden edifices. Newcomers confronted a host of unsanitary conditions such as torrential rains and open sewers, made worse by tropical illnesses that included malaria and dengue. To cater to the needs of oil workers, business interests opened makeshift storefronts, bars, casinos, and brothels that gradually acquired a degree of permanence. Faced with waves of immigrants and with few available services, daily activity acquired a degree of improvisation typical of bustling boomtowns. Although complaints from workers and nearby residents over these conditions proved common, Venezuela government officials largely ignored their requests and instead supported the foreign oil companies whenever they faced disputes.

The lack of sustained personal interaction among Venezuelans from different parts of the country further complicated relations in the oil fields. Except for earlier participation in nine-teenth century civil wars, the experience with oil represents the first time that large numbers of Venezuelans from distinct parts of the country actually came face to face with each other in a settled environment. The encounter between people from once-isolated states produced a profound cultural exchange that served to break down regional barriers. At another level, the interactions between Venezuelans from different parts of the country produced a new cultural *mestizaje* (miscegenation), as informal and formal relations produced new offspring between men and women from regions as diverse as Zulia, Lara, Mérida, and Trujillo in the west and Monagas, Anzoátegui, and Nueva Esparta in the east. Previously restricted by region and cultural mores, the communities near oil production now developed new sensibilities, temperaments, customs, and even dietary patterns.

By the late 1920s oil production expanded out of the state of Zulia and Falcón with the discovery of deposits in central and eastern Venezuela and became a truly national endeavor. Although strains remained evident, after an initial period of adjustment, life in the oilfields acquired a certain normalcy. Eager to stabilize operations, and hoping to avoid labor unrest, oil companies found it necessary to construct housing and provide basic services to their employees. Eventually the com-panies moved to create self-sustaining residential enclaves, known as *campos petroleros* (oil camps), with facilities segre-gated between their foreign and Venezuelan work forces. The contrast between a multiracial Venezuelan work force and a foreign white male skilled supervisorial staff accentuated prevailing US views on race, serving to confirm Venezuelan elites' views on these matters.

A marked difference existed between conditions for for-eigners and Venezuelans. Foreign employees lived in Senior Staff Camps, exclusive residential enclaves surrounded by fences and protected by *guachimanes* (a Venezuelan adaptation of watchmen), which as much as possible sought to reproduce life in the United States. As they evolved, the camps included not only houses, but also schools for children taught in English and Spanish and commissaries that offered an assortment of imported US goods. Foreign personnel also received medical services and had exclusive access to social clubs that included a cinema that screened Hollywood films and in most cases boasted swimming pools, tennis courts, baseball fields, and golf courses.

Venezuelan workers lived in separate *campos obreros* (workers' camps), areas built exclusively for local employees. Although they had access to subsidized food at a company commissary and some recreational facilities, their social clubs and schools were decidedly inferior. These stark differences exac erbated distinctions between US employees and Venezuelan workers who resented the special treatment afforded foreigners. However, at another level, it also highlighted differences between the Venezuelan employees of the powerful oil companies, who received the highest wages in the country, and the larger local population that lived in the shadow of the oil industry. These tangible differences remained a source of tension even after the industry was nationalized.

To ameliorate these distinctions, and faced by a relatively weak government, the foreign companies sometimes offered basic services to the neighboring Venezuelan communities including water, power, and in some cases, access to medical services. In many towns lacking services, a centrally located water faucet from the oil company provided for the town's needs, and people typically gathered the liquid in discarded oil or gasoline cans. Through these actions, the enterprises forged a web of relationships that projected the industry not only as a source of employment but also of social benefits.

Still, oil proved to be a mixed blessing for most ordinary Venezuelans. Promoted as the harbinger of modernization, it undoubtedly increased employment opportunities for thousands of oil workers and a small yet ambitious middle class and generated economic opportunities for business interests that catered to new consumers. For others directly in the path of the industry, however, it disrupted traditional patterns of rural and urban life. In decline even before the appearance of oil, agriculture suffered further neglect and by 1935 Venezuela became a net importer of food.

On the political front, oil did not introduce a new democratic order as some had anticipated but instead grafted itself onto the existing political structure. Thus opinions varied on the nature of the petroleum industry, depending upon its impact on different parts of the population. It did become clear, however, that the discovery of oil was an important watershed in the history of the country; Venezuelans could now distinguish a time before and a time after oil.

Who was Juan Vicente Gómez and how did he rule Venezuela for nearly three decades?

Juan Vicente Gómez was also an Andino from the state of Táchira on the border with Colombia. His personal formation reflected his early experiences on the hacienda La Mulera, his birthplace in 1857. Gómez's views on how to govern Venezuela drew in large measure on the notions of a patriarchal hierarchy, social relations, administrative skills, and interaction with foreigners typical of life at La Mulera and the coffee producing region of rural Táchira.

Facing declining health, in November 1908 President Castro traveled to Europe to seek medical treatment. In his capacity as Castro's military commander, Gómez enjoyed a reputation as a battle-tested leader and had gained the confidence of important sectors in and out of Venezuela. Having consulted with political allies, economic interests, military leaders, and the United States legation, Gómez had prepared for this moment for some time. He seized the presidency, and in a show of support, the United States and other European countries blocked Castro's efforts to return to Venezuela. Gómez quickly moved to consolidate power, assuring the allegiance of regional leaders and swiftly dealing with enemies. He went on to develop a network of governors and political bosses that did his bidding in most states.

Gómez also oversaw the expansion of a national military force, led by officers drawn mainly from his home state of Táchira to assure loyalty. Trained by foreign advisors and armed with modern weaponry, the military consisted of several divisions strategically placed throughout the country in order to quickly respond to any threats. Gómez also promoted the construction of a rudimentary highway system intended to connect western Venezuela with the rest of the country.

Gómez's rise to the presidency and the centralization of power signaled the end of an era in Venezuela as regional leaders were removed as arbiters in national politics. As a strong man, Gómez found a willing ally in the United States, which dispatched its navy and diplomats on several occasions in a show of support. Gómez became the first Venezuelan ruler not wholly dependent on internal forces to retain power. Under his rule, Washington absorbed Venezuela into its sphere of influence.

Before becoming president, Gómez had amassed a small fortune, monopolizing the sale of beef and liquor and establishing important connections to Venezuela's merchant class and foreign legations that had disliked Castro. While in power, he expanded his personal wealth to become the richest man in the country. He surrounded himself with positivist-minded urban intellectuals, who filled his cabinet and other government posts and readily defended his regime in and outside Venezuela. To protect the country's newfound position as an emerging petroleum exporter, Gómez inserted Venezuela in hemispheric affairs, tangling with oil-rich Mexico and usually siding with the United States on international matters. Fearing limits on their power, regional military strongmen initially led the opposition to Gómez; however, by 1915 most had been defeated, imprisoned, or exiled. Derided by his opponents as an illiterate, mixed-race peasant—or worse, as the illegitimate son of a Colombian—Gómez nonetheless managed to control Venezuela's fate for twenty-seven years.

Gómez did not rely solely on military might to stay in power, although he did not hesitate to resort to vicious repression if he felt threatened. Beyond the military, a network of informants in and out of Venezuela kept him abreast of potential threats. After prolonged periods of conflict, his slogan of "Union, Peace and Work" appealed to many, who viewed his rule as a guarantor of social peace. Additionally, his rise to power in 1908 coincided with favorable economic conditions for Venezuelan exports, and by 1914 the discovery of oil at Mene Grande provided the government with important new sources of revenue. With access to oil-generated resources, Gómez oversaw an expansion in the state apparatus and increased government spending on public works projects.

The Catholic Church recovered under Gómez the power it had lost under Castro; in fact, the Vatican awarded Gómez with a special honor for his services to the religion. Petroleum companies, such Standard Oil, also established an ongoing relationship with the Church, subsidizing the construction of churches near their oil camps and providing priests with living stipends and accommodations. Under the later years of the Gómez administration, the relations of power in Venezuela became analogous to a triumvirate made up of the government, the oil companies, and the Church.

Although he had cultivated ties with the economic elite, Gómez portrayed himself as an outsider, refusing to live in Caracas and instead taking up residence fifty miles away at an estate in the city of Maracay, where he received cabinet members, visitors, and foreign dignitaries. He eschewed the formal attire of the presidency and habitually dressed in a plain military uniform devoid of rank, insignia, or medals. He also nurtured paternalistic connections with ordinary Venezuelans, who regularly inundated him with personal requests for everything from a parcel of land, a pension for a widow, a sack of cement, or a source of employment.

What was Venezuela's experience with immigration following the discovery of oil?

Similar to most governments in Latin America during this period, the Gómez administration sought to attract European immigrants to Venezuela in order to increase (and more importantly, whiten) the population. Throughout the nineteenth century, governments had undertaken efforts to attract agricultural colonists to settle in Venezuela. Earlier, small numbers of Corsicans, Middle Easterners (especially Lebanese), and Italians had made their way to Venezuela. Canary Islanders, part of this earlier wave, and Spaniards from Galicia, Aragón, and the Basque country continued arriving over the next century, eventually constituting the most important wave of immigrants. Beginning in the 1870s, the first of many waves of Italian immigrants began to arrive, settling in the Andes and becoming important coffee producers. Portuguese immigrants followed Italians in number and importance.

Immigrants gradually dominated certain sectors of the economy in various parts of the country: Italians in construction and manufacturing, Portuguese in commerce, Canary Islanders in agriculture, and Middle Easterners in small-scale retail. Although many immigrants married Venezuelans and established families in the country, they also established regionally specific (Galician and Basque) social centers to celebrate their culture and ensure community solidarity. Despite the fact that immigrants dominated certain important economic arenas and publicly celebrated their culture, their presence in the country did not evoke a significant nationalist outcry.

During the last decades of the nineteenth century and the beginning of the twentieth century, however, the arrival of other non-European immigrants to Venezuela, specifically those of African descent, did evoke a nationalist and ethnically based response so strong that it challenged assumptions of racial equality. During this period, significant numbers of Afro-West

Indians, mostly from Trinidad and others from Guyana, began to work in mining and agriculture in eastern Venezuela and in the nascent oil industry in the west. Intellectuals and political figures, many of whom claimed European ancestry, quickly derided their presence and feared that they would introduce negative characteristics to the population.

By 1918, the government passed new laws affirming a ban on nonwhite immigrants. By the 1930s, one intellectual actually proposed the selective movement of people from Mérida, considered whiter, to Caracas to compensate for the larger population of people of color in the capital. During the remainder of the twentieth century, debates over "acceptable" and "unacceptable" immigrants revealed the extent to which racial difference and color continued to be important markers of social status in Venezuelan society. Gómez adeptly played to these racial fears, claiming to defend the country from "foreign" influences, though he enjoyed some for himself. For instance, Gómez endorsed a campaign to elevate the traditional harp-based music and dance of the *llanos* (plains) as the "national" music and dance, denouncing the growing popularity of "barbaric" Afro-Cuban popular dance music—the same music he featured in large parties at the presidential palace. This tension between the symbolic power of the modernity of European elite culture and the popularity and artistic power of African-based-and-influenced Venezuelan cultural forms has endured up to the present day.

What was the Generation of 1928 and who was Rómulo Betancourt?

By 1928, after twenty years in power, Gómez confronted new, unfamiliar opposition forces. Under the guise of student celebrations held during carnival festivities, university protestors took to the streets of Caracas, demanding an end to the regime. The students' pleas struck a responsive chord among multiple sectors of the Caracas population, now reaching 135,000, who joined their protest. Reflecting an eclectic mix of leftist and liberal ideas, the middle-class student leaders, subsequently dubbed the "Generation of 1928," included future leading figures in politics, culture, and the arts as well as significant numbers of women, who are usually excluded from these accounts.

Rómulo Betancourt became one of the key figures to emerge. Born in 1908 in Guatire, in the state of Miranda in the proximity of Caracas, he became a law student at the Universidad Central de Venezuela (Central University of Venezuela-UCV) and member of the Federación Estudiantil Venezolana (University Student Federation-FEV). Betancourt actively participated in organizing protests, leading to his arrest, incarceration, and eventually one of many exiles from the country. He and the other protagonists of the Generation of 1928 subsequently founded and led the democratic and leftist political parties that influenced the course of Venezuelan politics for most of the twentieth century.

Accustomed to dealing with his enemies on the battlefield, urban street protests represented a new challenge for Gómez. Fearing instability, he labeled the student leaders communists and had them imprisoned. Simultaneously authorities also faced a military uprising that sought to link up with student dissidents. Throughout Venezuela's history, disaffected military officers have often sought to establish relations with like-minded civilian groups. On this occasion, coordinated actions between disgruntled military officers and student leaders failed to achieve their objective, and authorities arrested most of the conspirators. Nonetheless, protests in various cities eventually compelled Gómez to release the students, suggesting the regime had not anticipated reactions from the population. Women took part in the street protests, organized support groups, produced and distributed publicity, raised funds, and performed clandestine activities in support of the protest. Eventually, the government exiled most student leaders in an attempt to debilitate the movement.

By the 1930s an aging Gómez began to cede power to his ministers; the most important symbol of this was the transfer of the military to General Eleazar López Contreras. A fellow Andean from Gómez's home state of Táchira, and a trusted high-ranking officer who had helped repress the 1928 rebellion, López Contreras enjoyed the support of Gómez's loyalists. The president retained power until December 17, 1935 when he died in his sleep after a prolonged illness. With his death some intellectuals asserted that Venezuela finally entered the twentieth century. They viewed the dictator as an aberration, rather than the product of historical events in Venezuela. Despite their hopes, the dictator's legacy would resonate and to some degree, negatively affect the future of Venezuela.

How did Venezuela change after Gómez's death?

As minister of defense, López Contreras, who ruled Venezuela between 1935 and 1941, had carefully prepared for Gómez's death, ensuring support within the military and the cabinet. Shortly after Gómez's death became public, violence erupted in many Venezuelan cities and in the western oil fields, where angry crowds killed several of Gómez's henchmen. Some members of the US expatriate community boarded oil tankers and awaited the arrival of troops from the safety of Lake Maracaibo. In Caracas, Eustoquio Gómez, the general's cousin, died in an altercation, his car burned by crowds and his bodyguards arrested.

The Gómez-controlled congress met shortly after his death and affirmed the decision taken earlier by the cabinet formally naming López Contreras as president. To gain popular support, López Contreras decreed a wage increase and ordered the demolition of a notorious Gómez-era prison where dissidents had been tortured. In the aftermath of Gómez's death, dozens of exiled political and student leaders, especially those who had taken part in the 1928 protests, returned to the country; others were released from jail.

To appease conservatives, and to maintain the apparatus of control, López Contreras allowed key Gómez era political leaders to maintain governorships and cabinet posts. Nonetheless, López Contreras's new cabinet initially incorporated an eclectic mix of people, some with ties to the Gómez era and some opposed to the old regime. Using the rising violence as a pretext, López Contreras also suspended civic and political guarantees, prohibited freedom of assembly, and imposed government censorship on the media.

Much had changed in Venezuela during Gómez's twenty-seven year rule. Venezuela, now with a population of over three million, had evolved from a fractured political entity disputed over by regional strongmen into a country with an emerging sense of identity and one of the largest oil reserves in the world, controlled largely by foreign interests. The petroleum industry and the profits it generated fueled growth in urban construction, giving rise to a new working class in the building trades. Caracas and other cities embodied a new dynamism, where traditions comingled within a new expanding urban landscape. Although buildings in the older parts of Caracas still lacked numbers, with street corners serving to identify the location of a house or an establishment, gradually multi-storied buildings began to replace the traditional red tile single-story ones that for decades had characterized Caracas.

While Caracas evolved, the countryside where the majority of the population still resided languished; illiteracy remained extremely high (some estimates ran as high as eighty percent) and poverty, tuberculosis, and tropical diseases extracted a heavy toll on a population whose life expectancy did not surpass thirty-three years. Outside of the oil-producing areas, basic services such as health care, education, electrical services and potable water proved scarce and most people eked out an existence by dividing their time working for landowners and producing their own basic foodstuffs. Under these conditions, migration to Caracas, the expanding network of secondary cities such as Maracaibo or Valencia, or the new emerging oilfields became an important option for many people. The pattern of rural to urban migration, begun during the 1930s, continued throughout the twentieth century.

How did López Contreras address new political demands?

Little wonder therefore that the period after the death of Gómez produced an unparalleled political effervescence: intellectuals issued proclamations and students organized a new national federation. Leftists and progressives coalesced into various organizations, and labor and public employees openly formed associations.

All of this began early in the López Contreras administration. Fearing that López Contreras would impose his own brand of dictatorship, moderates and leftist groups organized protests. In a scene unimaginable one year earlier, thousands marched on the presidential palace at Miraflores where López Contreras actually received the protestors. Recognizing the new political reality and the need to reach broad sectors of society, he became the first Venezuelan ruler to use radio to publicize his message. Within weeks, he restored some civil guarantees and made changes to his cabinet, all the while keeping the presidential prerogatives largely intact.

Seeking to placate the protesters López Contreras proposed new social and economic initiatives encompassed in what became known as the February Program, a series of limited reforms intended to modernize the state, largely unimaginable under Gómez. The López Contreras government introduced a five-year term limit on the presidency, created a national bank, introduced fiscal reform and municipal autonomy, increased road-building, restructured education, established labor laws, and initiated health and sanitation improvements. Opponents of the government remained divided and lacked unified objectives beyond these basic reforms, allowing López Contreras to skillfully preserve key elements of the old order and consolidate his hold on power on a new basis.

In 1936 Venezuela confronted its first national petroleum strike. Workers called for salary increases, equal treatment for Venezuelans and foreigners, and recognition of trade unions. The oil companies refused to concede, and the strike stretched on for forty-two days. Women played a key role in the strike, lending support, raising funds, and opening their homes to striking workers all over the country. In the end, although lower-paid workers received a slight pay increase, the López Contreras government physically repressed the strike and ordered laborers back to work. During the strike oil production declined nearly forty percent, meaning that state revenues also declined by a significant amount.

The lesson of the strike was not lost on future governments, which attempted to exert control over labor and its relations with the foreign oil companies. In February of 1937 López Contreras also declared all leftist and progressive parties illegal. The growth and importance of the labor force in petroleum was matched by the continued decline in agricultural production, and Venezuela was forced to continue importing food products to feed the nation.

What was the significance of new political forces that emerged in the mid-twentieth century?

As the López Contreras term neared its end at the start of World War II, new political forces and parties tested the waters, nominating novelist Rómulo Gallegos as a presidential candidate in 1941. Though the congress still selected the president, Venezuela witnessed active campaigning that incorporated women, who still did not have the right to vote but nonetheless held rallies and participated openly in the political process. Workers, the middle class, and other sectors also actively took sides between the two candidates, Gallegos and General Isaías Medina Angarita, yet another Andean officer.

In the end López Contreras's support for Medina Angarita (1941–1945) proved decisive and he assumed the presidency.

The Medina Angarita administration embodied the hope of some national elites that promoted the development of Venezuelan industry and agricultural self-sufficiency. The motto *"Sembrar Petroleo"* (Sowing Oil Profits), espoused by several intellectuals throughout the 1930s and adopted by the government, embodied the belief that Venezuela should employ oil profits to promote non-oil-related developments that would ultimately lessen dependence on petroleum revenues. This policy implied that the state would assume a greater role in the economy, promote infrastructure, subsidize national industries, and encourage agriculture, thus reducing dependence on imports. State-sponsored banks undertook major urban renovation projects altering the Caracas urban landscape, which now had a population of over 500,000. This policy also linked the interests of manufacturing and construction elites with those of the working class and allowed the state to serve as both promoter and arbiter of national interests. As unions grew in importance, this policy also generated increased competition between centrist and leftist parties for control of the new labor organizations.

How did World War II affect Venezuela?

Oil acquired new strategic importance with the outbreak of World War II. As a result, the Venezuelan government suspended constitutional rights in the oil fields. With Nazi submarines operating off the coast of Venezuela, attacking refineries on the nearby island of Aruba and sinking several tankers as they left Lake Maracaibo, the United States worried about the safety of oil installations and dispatched artillery units initially operated by American soldiers to protect coastal areas around Puerto La Cruz, Las Piedras on the Paraguaná Peninsula, and the island of Los Patos in the gulf of Paria off the coast of Trinidad. American military authorities acquiesced when their Venezuelan counterparts requested that no "Negro" soldiers be assigned to operate coastal batteries.

Because of the sinking of tankers by U-boats, crews of various ships threatened to mutiny and Venezuelan vessels began to operate at night and under the protection of convoys. Venezuela also granted the United States permission to use its airports as bases of operation to pursue submarines and an Army Air squadron operated out of Maracaibo. During this period Venezuela's armed forces received equipment and weapons under the US war era Lend Lease agreement.

Agents of the Federal Bureau of Investigation operating under the Special Intelligence Service (SIS) had started to work in Venezuela in October 1940, more than a year before Pearl Harbor; by 1943, with the United States fully engaged in the war, twenty-three agents had been stationed in the country assigned as liaisons to the United States embassy and consular offices. These agents prepared plans for the defense of oil installations, which they shared with the oil companies and the government for their implementation. The British and the United States jointly developed a list of supposed Axis sympathizers and the Venezuelan government closed down several businesses.

What was the importance of the 1943 oil legislation?

Despite the war, Venezuela had a new period of political freedom. The level of open political and social discourse proved unprecedented. The newly formed political parties, including *Acción Democrática* or AD founded in 1941, *Acción Nacional* or AC (1942) (a precursor to the Christian Democratic COPEI, founded in 1946), the *Union Popular* or UP (founded in 1944, representing communists) and the *Unión Republicana Democrática* (URD, founded in 1945) participated openly in municipal, regional, and national congressional elections. Founded in 1931, the Communist Party of Venezuela (PCV) had operated clandestinely or through front organizations, but by 1945 it acquired full legal status. Direct vote for the presidency still eluded Venezuelans, however.

On the international arena, Medina Angarita broke new ground, becoming the first Venezuelan president to travel abroad in 1943, visiting Colombia, Ecuador, Bolivia, and Peru (all regarded as Bolivarian States since Simón Bolívar participated in their independence); traveling to the United States; and establishing diplomatic relations with the Soviet Union.

Reforming the existing petroleum legislation became one of Medina Angarita's most enduring legacies. Even before approaching the issue he embarked on a national tour that took him to key oil camps where he held rallies and addressed workers' concerns. He approached the US and British oil companies, which initially resisted any efforts at altering the status quo. Frustrated by their response, Medina Angarita sent emissaries to meet with company officials in the United States as well as consult with the Roosevelt administration. With the World War as a backdrop, and fearing the potential of nationalization that had occurred in Mexico in 1938, the US government preferred a negotiated solution. In an environment of increasing nationalist rhetoric that promoted, among other issues, the hiring of more Venezuelans in administrative positions, the companies eventually acquiesced.

The oil reform of 1943 unified all previous legislation, ending a maze of earlier laws on the matter of oil and affirming the Venezuelan government's right to intervene in the industry. Venezuela had never relinquished ownership of the subsoil, so royalties and profit sharing were the only real issues debated. Royalties increased from 7 ½ percent to the new standard of 16 2/3 percent, and created the potential for a 60/40 sharing of profits once all taxes were calculated. After the 1945 coup, the new government ceded on this matter and employed the 50/50 formula for sharing profits, promoting the new arrangement as a "nationalist triumph," against foreign interests.

For its part, the government agreed not to question the validity of dubiously acquired Gómez-era oil titles and extend concessions until 1983. Opponents to the bill in the congress claimed that if the government had instead litigated the

Figure 3 Lake Maracaibo, 1940s. A major site of crude oil reserves, by the 1920s the lake had drawn more than a hundred foreign companies seeking to benefit from the oil bonanza.

validity of the titles, the oil companies would have been obligated to pay higher fees that could have been used to promote non-oil production. They also questioned the formula under which the government calculated royalties. Showing who wielded power in the country, however, Medina got the bill passed as proposed and it became law (Figure 3).

What was the state of race relations at mid-century?

In 1944, poet and political figure Andrés Eloy Blanco, a native of the western state of Sucre, which had a significant Afro-Venezuelan presence, coined the term *café con leche* (coffee with milk) to describe the Venezuelan racial makeup where widespread miscegenation had taken place. The coffee metaphor may not have been accidental. Over time, Venezuelans have devised so many ways of serving coffee that they parallel the country's racial heterogeneity. They range from *negro fuerte, normal* or *claro* (black strong coffee, normal or clear) to a *café marón,* (also *cortado) marón fuerte o claro,* (brown coffee strong, with milk or less milk), or a *café con leche, claro o oscuro* (with milk, clear, or dark), to the weakest formulation known as a *guayoyo* (very light) or even *tetero* (which contains little actual black coffee).

Eloy Blanco subsequently penned a classic poem, "Píntame Angelitos Negros" ("Paint Black Angels"), popularized by singers throughout Latin America, in which he pleaded with artists to include black angels next to the Western depiction of the Virgin Mary, typically surrounded by white cherubs. However, Eloy Blanco did not seem to believe that by blurring racial distinctions miscegenation had lessened racial difference. The concept of *café con leche* acquired widespread acceptance among intellectual circles, particularly in light-skinned middle- and upper-class sectors eager to dispel the notion that racial prejudice still existed.

Except for immigration policy, which, as in most Latin American countries, deliberately restricted people of color, no formal laws dictated racial segregation. Concealed as cultural and social norms, divisive racial practices became visible when publicly transgressed. In 1945, several hotels, including the recently inaugurated Avila (built with funds provided by Nelson Rockefeller) on Jorge (George) Washington Avenue, initially constructed to house visiting foreign oil officials, refused service to several US African American performers visiting Caracas. Jim Crow had gone further south.

Who replaced Medina Angarita?

By the end of 1944 Medina Angarita entered into discussions with the various political forces to select his successor. Fearing a conservative backlash, Medina proved unwilling to alter the constitution and institute direct universal suffrage in the election of the presidency. As a result, the senate continued

to determine the selection of the president. The political liber-
alization under Medina had generated an unsettled political
environment. Medina never secured the support of the officer corps and inherited a divided military. Factions became
evident in the military among those who supported López
Contreras, a small faction that sided with Medina, and a new
bloc composed of younger academy-trained junior officers
who resented the power of the older Andean hierarchy and
complained about promotions and low salaries in the armed
forces.

Others sectors had also begun to mobilize. By 1944, several
thousand women had signed petitions demanding the right to
vote. Reforms to the constitution in 1945 finally allowed women
to vote for town councils. Surprisingly, conservative Diógenes
Escalante, the Venezuelan ambassador to Washington and former Minister of the Interior, whom López Contreras had considered in 1941, emerged as a consensus candidate. Rómulo
Betancourt, who as we've seen was one of the founders of
Acción Democrática and a leading member of the Generation
of 1928, actually flew to Washington to convince the waver-
ing Escalante to accept the position. Before he could do so,
however, Escalante became seriously ill, and Medina selected
Angel Biaggini, his Minister of Agriculture, creating a rupture
with the newly formed political parties.

Within the military, disgruntled younger officers, organized under the banner of the Unión Patriótica Militar or
UPM, began to prepare for a coup. After developing their
plans, and cognizant of the new democratic aspirations of
the country, they approached the leaders of AD who agreed
to participate in the planned coup. In October 1945 they put
their plan into action and toppled Medina, who resigned as
president. A "Revolutionary Junta" that included Betancourt,
the president of AD, four other civilians, and two military officers assumed control of the country. When confronted with
opposition in the states of Zulia, Táchira, and Falcon, they
threatened to use force to subdue them. The United States

embassy in Caracas recommended that Washington recognize the new junta.

What was the Trienio (1945–1948) and what is its legacy in Venezuela?

The *trienio*—or three-year period—refers to the years between the ouster of Medina on October 18, 1945 and the coup against the democratically elected president Rómulo Gallegos in November 24, 1948. The leaders of the so-called "October Revolution" proposed to establish a US-style democracy while publicly heralding their opposition to communism. For two of the three years that Acción Democrática governed Venezuela, it shared power with the young officers of the UPM. Under their power-sharing arrangement, Betancourt served as the president; Lieutenant Colonel Carlos Delgado Chalbaud, who attended military school in Paris, became the minister of defense; and Marcos Pérez Jiménez served as military chief of staff. Military budgets nearly tripled during the *trienio*. Oil industry and United States embassy officials feared that the Communist Party could make inroads in the politically charged climate. The foreign oil companies formed an "Industrial Security Council" to coordinate security with the American embassy and its military attaches.

Shortly after the coup in 1945, the leading foreign oil companies in Venezuela met with Betancourt and received assurances that little would change in their relations with the government. To avoid a situation like that in Mexico, where the government had nationalized foreign oil investments in 1938, the companies agreed to relatively mild reforms in order to protect their investments. Despite efforts to portray themselves as nationalist reformers, AD did not fundamentally alter relations with the oil companies. In fact, once in office, they left intact the 1943 Oil Law that they had originally opposed.

AD moved quickly to address important social and economic issues, continuing plans begun by Medina Angarita while also implementing new efforts at agrarian reform, educational change, eradicating tropical disease, promoting immigration, expanding infrastructure, and encouraging manufacturing. A new electoral law assigned each party an official color and symbol, as illiteracy remained a persistent problem. AD took white, COPEI green, the Communists red, and the recently formed URD yellow.

The political mobilization introduced during the *trienio* compelled existing political and social forces to redefine their role in society. Across the political spectrum labor unions, students, women, rural populations, the military, the Church, economic interests, and the four main political parties competed for power. Newspapers carried the debates of the day The Communist Party competed with the *adecos* (members of AD) for control of labor unions, especially in the powerful oil workers union. American officials cultivated relations with the more conservative forces in the junta, forging common ground in their desire to curb the influence of the communists in the oil workers unions. The Catholic Church hierarchy, long accustomed to a cozy relationship with those in power, worried about the promotion of secular education and a possible curtailment of their privileged position if the Left gained power.

In June 1947 delegates to a constitutional convention dominated overwhelmingly by Acción Democrática reaffirmed the principle of universal suffrage and women's right to vote. Radio stations broadcast the congressional debates live, drawing impressive audiences that competed with the popular radio soap operas. Taking advantage of its position of power, AD expanded its national apparatus and gradually became the nation's leading party. Part of AD's strategy had been to promote the development of party-controlled labor federations, expand the state apparatus, and establish links to business organizations to increase its reach in society.

After two years, with political pressure building, the junta ceded power and elections for president took place in December of 1947. Rómulo Betancourt by this point had earned the enmity of multiple sectors, including the military, and opted not to promote his own candidacy.

Who was Romulo Gallegos and why is he so important in postwar Venezuela?

Rómulo Gallegos, born in Caracas in 1884, was the author of works such as *Doña Bárbara* and *Canaima*, as well as a leading political figure in Venezuela's emerging democracy at mid-century. Many of his novels—still popular in Venezuela and Latin America—draw inspiration from the social and cultural challenges Venezuela faced as it made the transition from a rural agricultural to an increasingly urban, oil-producing nation that struggled to balance traditional customs with the pressures of modernity.

In Venezuela's first free and direct election in December of 1947, Gallegos, running as Acción Democrática's candidate, won by a landslide. Delgado Chalbaud retained the position of Minister of Defense. Gallegos's victory and the broader process underway in Venezuela compelled intellectuals, artists, and folklorists to begin to define the cultural and artistic expression of an emerging Venezuelan identity. As part of the festivities associated with Gallegos's inauguration, poet Juan Liscano and others organized the *Fiestas de la Patria* (Celebrations of the Nation) at the Nuevo Circo, a Caracas bullring, drawing together the various regional expressions of Venezuelan culture and attempting to weave them into a new national narrative. One writer labeled the event a "spiritual discovery," since it represented the first time that many residents of Caracas witnessed the diversity of cultural experiences that existed in Venezuela outside the capital city.

Although Gallegos had won the election by over seventy percent, internal dissent continued after he took power and his government confronted a turbulent political landscape.

Acción Democrática actions began to worry the more conservative sectors of society, including the Church and business interests. The military demanded that AD create a bipartisan cabinet, and claimed that the party was seeking to create its own militia and stockpile weapons. Former president López Contreras and dictator Rafael Trujillo of the Dominican Republic began circulating rumors of a possible coup. As tensions mounted, officers who had participated in the *trienio* presented Gallegos with a list of concerns over his government's actions, including the forced departure of Betancourt from the country, whom they accused of retaining power. When Gallegos rebuked their demand, the very officers that helped AD come to power in 1945 put an end to the democratic experiment on November 24, 1948, overthrowing Gallegos and exiling him. Gallegos took up residence in Mexico.

Gallegos initially blamed the United States and the oil companies for sanctioning the coup. While the large oil companies such as Creole (Standard Oil) and the United States embassy had nurtured relations with AD and did not especially stand to gain much from a coup, the presence of US military attaché Colonel Edward F. Adams and a US civilian, Robert T. Brinsmade, in the country just as the Venezuelan officers were planning the coup suggests that they may have worked at cross-purposes from the embassy and the oil companies. Some assert that although Betancourt had won the confidence of the State Department and the oil companies, the Pentagon, which viewed oil as a strategic reserve in any future conflict, did not trust either Betancourt or Acción Democrática and had engineered the coup against Gallegos.

Who was Marcos Pérez Jiménez and how did he come to power?

Following the overthrow of Gallegos, Lieutenant Colonel Carlos Delgado Chalbaud headed the new junta, which also included the former military Chief of Staff during the *trienio*, Colonel Marcos Pérez Jiménez, and a politician. The junta outlawed AD and the Communist Party, arresting and expelling some of its leaders.

With Acción Democrática's leaders in exile, the Communist Party decried the coup and organized clandestine resistance. In 1950, Delgado Chalbaud was killed during a purported botched kidnapping attempt; his assassin likewise perished in an escape attempt. With Delgado Chalbaud out of the picture, Pérez Jiménez consolidated his position within the junta and emerged as the leader of the military and eventually the nation. Many people continue to believe that Pérez Jiménez orchestrated Delgado Chalbaud's death to advance his career, although no conclusive evidence linked him to the assassination. The junta proposed elections in November of 1952. Many cast their vote for the most progressive candidate in a much-narrowed field, Jovito Villalba (URD) and when it appeared Villalba would win, the military falsified the results and declared Pérez Jiménez president.

The rise of Pérez Jiménez symbolized both continuity and a break with the tradition established by Andean generals, who had ruled Venezuela since 1898. Like his predecessors he was born in the Andean state of Táchira in 1914, but unlike them he had trained in professional military academies, including in Peru, where he became close to junior military officers who espoused nationalist views but opposed leftist groups such as the Communist Party. In fact, the United States embassy expressed concern about the ascent of Pérez Jiménez, fearing that he would be a populist whom they couldn't control, like Juan Perón of Argentina. However, Pérez Jiménez and the United States quickly found common ground on the matter of oil policy and anticommunism. Nonetheless, as early as 1951, framed by a nationalist rhetoric, Pérez Jiménez spoke of a new *Ideal Nacional* (National Ideal) that proposed modernizing the nation, its infrastructure, its physical space, and even its entire society.

What kind of advances did Venezuela make in the 1950s?

Pérez Jiménez assumed power at a propitious time. Washington's Cold War doctrine favored governments, democratic or not, that controlled challenges from left wing social reformers. In 1954, to show its support, the Eisenhower administration awarded Pérez Jiménez the Legion of Merit, the highest award given to a foreign dignitary by the United States government. The conflict in Korea and the efforts to nationalize oil in Iran had increased demands for Venezuelan oil, allowing the government to reap substantial profits. Increased revenue permitted it to implement its grandiose *Nuevo Ideal Nacional* (New National Ideal). One goal was to improve the access to Caracas from the Caribbean coast, which meandered over an arduous and dangerous mountain route. By 1953 construction concluded on a superhighway that linked the capital to the port city of La Guaira and the international airport at Maiquetia. By mid-decade an aerial tramway connected Caracas to the Ávila Peak that overlooks the city. From here city residents could—and still can—admire views of the Caribbean and the city below. In the western Andean state of Mérida, construction began on the longest aerial tram in the world, connecting the city below to Pico Bolívar at an altitude of over 16,000 feet.

During the 1950s, construction projects reached new levels. The boom transformed the Caracas skyline and its population now included over 700,000 residents. Rural migrants to Caracas continued to set up residences on the hillsides and ravines that surround the capital, building fragile structures euphemistically known as *ranchos* (shacks). By 1957 the population of Venezuela hovered at close to seven million, a significant number of which resided in urban areas. To address the perennial problem of housing, the government funded extensive apartment complexes, known as *super bloques*, in western Caracas within site of the presidential palace. They also allocated funds for the dramatic expansion of the national university, museums, sports complexes (especially baseball fields), and public hospitals.

New high-rise office buildings dotted the urban landscape and new residential zones known as *urbanizaciones* extended the limits of Caracas's urban reach. A new transit system comprising boulevards and highways linked the various neighborhoods of the city, with southern and eastern Caracas becoming the preferred residential sites for the middle and upper-middle classes. Modern cliffside homes confirmed the process of change taking place. By the mid-1950s Delta, Pan-American, and Eastern Airlines offered service between Caracas and Miami and other US cities.

Part of the point of the *ideal nacional* was, of course, to help define what it meant to be Venezuelan, and it arrived at a moment of heightened immigration. Historically, Venezuela's attempt to attract European immigrants had met with very limited success. This changed with the end of the war in Europe and the expansion of the Venezuelan economy during the *trienio*, which created conditions for an influx of immigrants. The Pérez Jiménez administration openly promoted the immigration of thousands of Italians, Spaniards, and Portuguese in order to alter the country's racial makeup. Addressing the issue of immigration and race in an interview, Pérez Jiménez asserted "European immigration during the 1950s did not happen by chance, it was very calculated. . . . It was necessary to improve the ethnic component . . . to improve the race."[1] The arrival of several thousand Europeans swelled the ranks of existing groups, settling mostly in existing urban areas. The military government saw the immigrants as potential allies. In addition to Europeans, Venezuela also attracted a significant Colombian migration that continued throughout much of the later decades of the twentieth century. As they prepared for elections in 1952, authorities sought to register immigrants in order to gain an electoral advantage.

Local elites, or *"criollo* capitalists" as one critic labeled them—especially those in construction, imports, and commerce—benefited tremendously from lucrative government contracts and the expansion of markets. Many government public works contracts went to European construction companies that paid *comisiones*, inducements—or, less politely, bribes—as part of the cost of doing business with the government. To ensure support from the military, the government constructed an opulent military facility, the *Círculo Militar*, while also providing funds to send officers to study abroad; for example, officials of the Seguridad Nacional—SN (National Security), founded during the *trienio*, received anti-subversion training in the United States. Other public works undertaken by the government included a publicly owned steel mill in the state of Bolívar, a petrochemical plant in Zulia, a major dam and irrigation project in Guárico, a shipyard in Puerto Cabello, and a hydroelectric plant on the Caroní River. Two five-star hotels, the *Tamanaco* and the *Lago*, both catering to foreigners, opened respectively in Caracas and in Maracaibo.

While grandiose projects in the spirit of the *ideal nacional* altered the physical landscape of cities such as Caracas and Maracaibo, they did little to address the growing conditions of inequality evident in Venezuelan society. Outside of the oil industry, conditions in the countryside remained bleak, fueling migration to the urban centers where access to some social services served to mitigate conditions of inequality, thus swelling the ranks of the urban poor. Increasingly two Venezuelas took shape: one that benefitted from the oil economy, and the other that lived in the shadow of the industry, for which conditions had not fundamentally changed. These two realities competed within the same national boundaries; one was a modern oil-producing nation closely allied to the United States, and the other a Latin American country where exports, even one as strategic as oil, had failed to solve the persistent problems of poverty and inequality for a large majority of the population. Yet despite issues with inequality, most people expressed optimism about the future and expected conditions for their children to improve.

During the last week of November of 1957, an incident with American jazz great Louis Armstrong in Caracas demonstrated how little social and racial conditions had advanced. Armstrong and other jazz musicians often traveled abroad at the behest of the State Department, which used music as a tool of cultural diplomacy, aimed at isolating the Soviet Union during the Cold War. Armstrong arrived in Caracas during the last week of November to perform at the UCV (Central University) and appear on a television show. A performance at a public arena that drew only scant crowds disappointed Armstrong. After having been critical about events surrounding integration efforts in Little Rock, Arkansas, during his stay in Caracas he praised the progress the United States had been making on race relations. To his surprise, when he attempted to check into the Tamanaco Hotel, operated by Intercontinental—at the time a subsidiary of Pan Am—he was denied a room. Venezuelan accounts of the event took great pains to highlight that the hotel was part of a US chain; however the reality is that the policies reflected prevailing Jim Crow racial practices evident in both countries.

How did resistance to Pérez Jiménez develop?

Efforts to open the nation up to democracy took various forms. While its principal leaders went into exile, some of Acción Democrática's adherents initially took up arms against the Pérez Jiménez regime, subsequently opting to boycott the 1952 election. To ensure stability, the government increasingly relied on the Seguridad Nacional (SN)—the political police—and its director, Pedro Estrada. The SN developed an intelligence network that overlapped with the security departments of the major foreign oil companies. Rank-and-file party members of Acción Democrática and the Communist Party began to cooperate in their actions against the regime; by mid-1957 URD and Christian Democrats joined their efforts, leading to the creation of the Junta Patriótica (Patriotic Front) to coordinate opposition to the government. Discontent also developed within the armed forces, as younger officers witnessed a decline in promotional opportunities. Some in the military also complained that the Seguridad Nacional usurped their power and, in some cases, infiltrated their ranks.

The catalyst for the ouster of Pérez Jiménez came in 1957, when he attempted to extend his rule through a plebiscite. The Junta Patriótica called for an end to reelections and for a democratic government that respected civil liberties. Considering his somewhat nationalist rhetoric and efforts to procure arms from European suppliers, in the end even the United States expressed doubts about Pérez Jiménez.

Students at the UCV, Venezuela's largest public university, declared a strike on November 21, 1957, and formed brigades that went out throughout the city. On January 1, 1958, Colonel Hugo Trejo and some other officers declared an open rebellion against the government. Although the uprising failed, air force officers also joined in the revolt, exposing serious fractures in the military. Trejo's proposal to democratize the armed forces and integrate their actions with the larger population continued to reverberate among younger officers. His actions underscored the presence of nationalist and radical thought within elements of the Venezuelan officer corps.

On January 10, another group of officers presented Pérez Jiménez with a list of demands, leading to the resignation of key members of his government, including Estrada, the hated director of the Seguridad Nacional. The Junta Patriótica called for a general strike on January 21 that mobilized broad sectors of society, and the military refused to repress the assembled crowds. On January 23, realizing that he had lost the support of the military, Pérez Jiménez went into exile in Miami.

As official order collapsed, angry crowds turned on members of the hated Seguridad Nacional and their informants, beating some and publicly executing others. Protestors set fire to the offices of the SN, torched the offices of a pro-government newspaper, and sacked Pérez Jiménez's home. The officers who had rebelled against Pérez Jimenez organized a "Junta de Gobierno" under the leadership of Admiral Wolfgang Larrazabal, and journalist Fabricio Ojeda, a member of URD, emerged as leader of the Junta Patriótica. The presence of two former military officers sympathetic to the dictator on the Junta de Gobierno generated protests, however, and forced their resignation and replacement by civilians.

What was the Pacto de Punto Fijo?

The *Pacto de Punto Fijo* refers to a document signed by the leaders of Venezuela's non-communist parties—Betancourt (AD), Caldera (COPEI), and Villalba (URD)—that sought to minimize public interparty rivalry, avoid efforts by the military to exploit political divisions, and curtail the role of the left, which had been critical to the ouster of Pérez Jiménez. The pact takes its name from Caldera's home in Caracas, where the meeting took place. The outline of the Pacto de Punto Fijo had been established at an earlier meeting attended by the exiled leaders in New York.

Betancourt had used his time in exile wisely, building strong ties with US labor leaders, public figures, members of Congress, and the State Department to promote his liberal, democratic, but anticommunist credentials. Nonetheless, he and the other two leaders had been out of the country as the resistance to Pérez Jiménez had unfolded and the Communist Party had assumed a significant role. A younger generation of leaders from the traditional parties had actively cooperated with the communists. Other sectors in society also had mobilized, including intellectuals, journalists, public school teachers, high school students, and even merchants. The radicalization of any post-Pérez Jiménez government concerned the US oil companies, the State Department, and the more conservative leaders of the AD and COPEI.

Faced with these conditions, the adherents to the Pacto agreed to promote political peace, respect the outcome of popular elections, and incorporate losing parties in their cabinets. At the same time they ratified antidemocratic measures that deliberately excluded left-wing parties from the political process. Political forces active in the resistance against Pérez Jiménez charged that the pact consolidated the power of the traditional parties and its three leaders. Many Venezuelans referred to the power sharing arrangement as a government by the "Holy Trinity."

The months between the ouster of Pérez Jiménez and the election proved tense as rumors of possible coups circulated frequently. Fearing the impact of Colonel Trejo on the armed forces, the government appointed him as ambassador to Costa Rica to facilitate his departure from the country. In May of 1958, President Eisenhower dispatched Vice-President Nixon on a goodwill tour of Latin America. American support for military dictatorships, as well as US involvement in the 1954 coup in Guatemala that had led to the ouster of the democratically elected president, sparked protests during Nixon's visit to the region. Hundreds of demonstrators in Caracas attacked Nixon's motorcade, and the Eisenhower government dispatched a US Navy warship. Nixon cut his visit short, unable to deposit flowers at Bolívar's tomb or meet with the country's leaders. While Betancourt, Caldera, and Villalba condemned the protest, Larrazabal expressed some sympathy with the cause of the protestors. The United States increasingly became concerned about the radicalization occurring in Venezuela and the eventual outcome of elections.

What was the outcome of Venezuela's 1958 democratic elections?

After so many years of dictatorship, a democratic election captured the attention of the nation. One woman in the eastern state of Bolívar who gave birth to triplets named her boys in honor of the three candidates: Rafael, Rómulo, and Wolfgang. Strong support existed for a unity ticket headed by Larrazabal, and early polling indicated he might win the election. Elections on December 7, 1958 produced a different outcome, however, ratifying Betancourt as president of Venezuela. Although residents of Caracas soundly rejected Betancourt, votes from rural areas, where Acción Democrática had built up a strong party apparatus, assured his victory. As it became evident that Betancourt would win, rioting broke out in Caracas on December 8 and protestors attempted to storm the electoral council where officials counted votes.

Betancourt's previous efforts to court key US constituents paid dividends. The US delegation to his inauguration included the American political activist and scholar Robert J. Alexander, supporter Frances Grant, journalist Herbert Matthews, head of the AFL-CIO George Meany, and Oregon Democratic congressman Charles Porter, whom the *New York Times* had labeled "Venezuela's unofficial ambassador in Washington." Labeled "the mellowed revolutionary" by the *New York Times* after the election, Venezuela acquired heightened status in US policy toward Latin America. At his inauguration Betancourt (1959–1964) proclaimed that the "philosophy of Communism is not compatible with the development of Venezuela." Cuba's overthrow of its US-supported dictatorship in 1959 and the ensuing nationalization of foreign industries drew Washington's ire. As uneasiness over Cuba grew, Venezuela increasingly became a showcase for a mildly reformist, yet stridently anticommunist government that served as a trusted US ally during the Cold War.

What challenges did Betancourt confront?

In office, Betancourt immediately confronted a great number of challenges. These included rebellions by right-wing military officers, an assassination attempt (in which Rafael Trujillo of the Dominican Republic was implicated), and attacks from the left for the adoption of austerity measures and opposition to the Cuban Revolution. Shortly after Betancourt's election,

Fidel Castro visited Caracas, drawing throngs to all the events in which he participated. Betancourt's move to the right had angered many of the younger Acción Democrática members who had fought against Pérez Jiménez and now expected reforms. Joined by a handful of former leaders, in May of 1960 they bolted from AD and formed the *Movimiento de Izquierda Revolucionaria*—MIR (Left Revolutionary Movement). Other discontented *adecos* also eventually left the party and formed different organizations. As Betancourt increasingly began to govern with a heavy hand, the MIR determined that conditions in the country merited an armed insurrection to overturn the government. Facing a worker's strike, Betancourt suspended constitutional liberties, a tactic that he used often during his administration.

Disillusionment with the course of Venezuelan politics increased within the country. In 1962, Fabricio Ojeda, the former leader of the Junta Patriótica and an elected deputy in the Venezuela Congress, gave an address in which he cited a litany of repressive moves taken by the Betancourt government. He insisted that little had changed with the ouster of Pérez Jiménez and announced to his colleagues that he would resign his position and join the growing armed insurgency that had formed against the government.

By 1962 bloody rebellions, some that included dissident leftist military officers, had erupted in Carupano in the east and in the west central port of Puerto Cabello. The turbulent climate and open attacks on the Communist Party by the government led the party to join the armed insurrection. By 1962, the MIR, the PCV, elements of the URD, and students from the UCV were engaged in guerrilla war against the government. Eventually, the insurgents united under the banner of the *Fuerzas Armadas de Liberación Nacional* or FALN (Armed Forces of National Liberation). Although they engaged in several violent actions, including the bombing of the Sears store in Caracas and the kidnapping of a US officer, they failed to generate a mass following.

Despite a rise in repression by Betancourt's AD, the left had misread conditions in the country and the willingness of the population, especially in the rural areas (where Betancourt's support was still solid), to join an armed revolt. The military, supported by US Green Beret advisors and its own military intelligence branch (SIFA), successfully confronted the armed insurgency and increased protection of oil production sites. The Ministry of the Interior, under Carlos Andres Pérez, also used all the forces at their disposal. This included the newly formed Dirección General de Policía or DIGEPOL (General Police Directorate) that replaced the feared Seguridad Nacional, creating a national police force that at times operated without great concern for the law.

Besides leftist insurgents, the Caracas city government also faced a growing crime rate. During the first half of 1962, the city, with a population of over 1.2 million, recorded 6,600 cases of assault and robbery, with over one thousand people being shot. Venezuelan officials contracted Chilean advisors to train officers, increased the police force to seven thousand, and created a special detail to guard banks, a frequent target of criminals. By 1963, to curb the proliferation of weapons and address the increase in crime, police forces were placed under the authority of a military commander.

While prosecuting the war against the insurgents, Betancourt also began to consolidate his position. He nurtured a patronage system that came to characterize Acción Democrática's relations with labor, business interests, and segments of the rural population. Betancourt also moved to buttress relations with the Catholic hierarchy, despite the fact that key elements of the Church had earlier supported Pérez Jiménez. He endorsed a pact between management and workers that hamstrung unions and limited strikes, promoted a land reform act that in theory limited the size of estates, and pursued moderate nationalist economic policies to help local manufacturing while boosting state oil revenues. Efforts to impose taxes on foreign goods such as imported Scotch whiskey and American cigarettes gave rise to a lucrative contraband trade in these goods.

Refusing to nationalize the industry, Betancourt's policies on oil mirrored those of earlier regimes and administrations, essentially refusing to grant new concessions while maximizing existing revenue streams. Since the late 1940s, the Venezuelan government had begun to consider the consequences of increasing competition between oil-producing countries and dispatched a delegation to Iraq, Iran, and Saudi Arabia. By 1959, facing dropping oil prices and recognizing the importance of concerted action, Minister of Hydrocarbons Juan Pablo Pérez Alfonzo met with other Middle East and Persian producers in Cairo. During 1960, the group convened in Baghdad and founded the Organization of Petroleum Exporting Countries (OPEC), with Venezuela as a founding member.

How was Venezuela governed under the Punto Fijo pact?

Elections in 1963, boycotted by the left, produced another victory for Acción Democrática as Raúl Leoni, a former minister of labor during the *trienio*, assumed the presidency succeeding Betancourt. In the wake of its multiple internal splits, AD received only thirty-three percent of the vote and again relied on support from rural areas to win the election in a crowded field of six candidates. Acción Democrática's inability to make inroads in Caracas, with its expanding population and disproportionate influence in the country, represented a significant challenge for the party. More importantly, however, the election of Leoni in 1963 symbolized the first time in Venezuelan history that one elected president transferred power peacefully to another. In 1964, *Newsweek* ran a picture of Leoni on its cover superimposed over an image of Fidel Castro with the headline "Latin America, the Promise and the Threat."

Leoni continued to implement many of Betancourt's policies. The new government continued to rely on oil revenues to spur local manufacturing, especially in the automotive, chemicals, and electronic sectors. Construction also began on a major hydroelectric project across the Caroni River known as the Guri Dam (today the Simón Bolívar Hydroelectric Project), which eventually supplied a significant portion of Venezuela's electrical needs. The project decreased dependence on oil and instead created a dependence on the flow of tropical rivers to produce energy, with the unfounded anticipation that traditional rainfall amounts would persist unchanged into the future. The Six Day War of 1967 in the Middle East boosted Venezuelan oil exports. None of these actions, however, diminished the growing divide between the middle and upper sectors of the population and the ever-expanding urban poor.

The small but persistent insurgency of leftist forces fighting against the government remained unresolved and on several occasions Leoni suspended constitutional guarantees and reaffirmed his commitment to crush the opposition. One tactic included the creation of specialized counterinsurgency units stationed in specific theaters of operations. Extensive human rights abuses started to become commonplace. For many, the case of Alberto Llovera, a scholar and communist arrested by the Dirección General de Policía in October of 1965, became emblematic of the repression. His body, bearing signs of torture and wrapped in chains, subsequently surfaced on a beach in eastern Venezuela. The purported jailhouse suicide of Fabricio Ojeda, the former Unión Republicana Democrática legislator, in June of 1966 also raised concerns. By the late 1960s, the Communist Party began to reconsider the merits of the armed struggle and by 1967 decided instead to look for peaceful ways to reclaim its status as a legal party.

Did the election of Rafael Caldera alter how Venezuela was ruled?

During elections held on December 1, 1968, COPEI's three-time candidate, Rafael Caldera, narrowly won the presidency.

Serious internal division within Acción Democrática aided Caldera's victory. As the campaign unfolded, AD leaders had expelled longtime party stalwart Luis Beltran Prieto Figueroa. He founded the *Movimiento Electoral del Pueblo*-MEP (People's Electoral Movement), severely crippling AD. Under the banner of Unión para Avanzar or UPA ("Forward in Union") the Communist Party also nominated candidates for Congress, although they received less than three percent of the vote.

In office, Caldera kept his electoral promise and granted amnesty to any insurgent who agreed to demobilize. By 1969, the Communist Party accepted government conditions and became a legal opposition party. Subsequently, division within the Communist Party gave way to a new organization, the *Movimiento al Socialismo* or MAS (Movement toward Socialism), paralleling the electoral strategy pursued in Europe by Communist parties. By 1973, the *Movimiento de Izquierda Revolucionaria*, or MIR, suffered a series of internal divisions and its members slowly reintegrated into civilian life. After 1973, only one major guerrilla front continued operations in rugged western Venezuela. By the end of the Caldera administration the majority of the organized left had made the transition from an insurrectionist to a more conventional strategy, taking up instead the task of community organizing while others actively participated in the electoral arena.

The Caldera administration faced lingering frustration over unaddressed reforms, wages, and social conditions. Throughout 1969 and 1970, the government confronted student protests, including some from a radical youth wing of COPEI. Protest quickly spread to other universities and included high school students. Like Leoni before him, Caldera sent troops to confront students at the UCV, violating its status as an autonomous institution. To distance himself from past policies and proposing to confront the persistent issue of crime, Caldera issued a presidential decree creating the *Dirección Nacional de los Servicios de Inteligencia y Prevención* or DISIP

(National Intelligence and Prevention Services) to replace the much-despised Dirección General de Policía.

Demanding wage increases, teachers went on strike in late 1969. Health workers also demanded higher wages. Not long after, workers at the national iron and steel mill also laid down their tools. Protests and strikes reached levels not seen since the struggle to oust Pérez Jiménez and continued throughout much of Caldera's term in office.

Political activism not only addressed national concerns but protested US policy in Vietnam. In fact, fearing a repeat of the street protests that marked Nixon's visit to Venezuela in 1958, Caldera asked Nelson Rockefeller, traveling throughout Latin America on a goodwill mission, to cancel his visit to the country in 1969. Besides oil and commercial interests, Rockefeller owned *Monte Sacro*, a large estate in central Venezuela where he often vacationed. Interestingly, while the presence of American dignitaries evoked nationalist responses, American oil companies failed to illicit such reactions. This underscores the extent to which the US oil companies had managed to integrate themselves into the Venezuelan political and social landscape.

On many levels, the Caldera presidency reflected continuity with the two previous administrations. While the Punto Fijo agreement assured peaceful transition of power, it also gave rise to client/patron relations and raised concerns of corruption. The popular adage in Venezuela *"no me des, ponme donde hay"* ("place me where I can help myself") underscored the notion that a government position could generate additional earnings. The practice of paying *comisiones* (bribes) as the price of doing business with the government continued unabated. As the state increased its percentage of oil profits, corruption became endemic and entrenched.

Without a majority in the national Congress, Caldera forged alliances with other parties. The government lent its support to a proposal by the *Movimiento Electoral del Pueblo* to national-ize the natural gas industry. Concerned about the impending expiration of petroleum concessions, it approved a reversion law to protect the value of the industry's infrastructure. At the end of 1971 the congress also approved Decree 832 that increased the power of the Ministry of Hydrocarbons over foreign companies, forcing them to submit plans for exploration, production, and sales to the government for approval. Predictably the US press decried the legislation. With concessions set to expire in the near future, Decree 832 raised the spectre that the industry might eventually be nationalized.

What was the Gran Venezuela Project?

The presidential elections of December 1973 pitted two former ministers of the interior against each other. Acción Democrática-nominated Carlos Andrés Pérez, born in 1922 in the state of Táchira who had been Betancourt's personal secretary and the Minister of the Interior, responsible for security forces during the violent periods of the 1960s. COPEI put forth Lorenzo Fernández, a relatively lackluster candidate who endured a bruising battle at his party's convention and in the press before receiving the nomination. Fernández promised continuity with the Caldera government, while Pérez— nicknamed *el gocho*, a reference to his Andean roots—played to his more dynamic and flamboyant character. The election proved contentious, both candidates spent substantial sums of money and retained the services of US campaign professionals, a trend that increased with each succeeding presidential campaign.

Two left-wing candidates, Jesús Paz Galarraga from the *Movimiento Electoral del Pueblo* and José Vicente Rangel of the *Movimiento al Socialismo*, also contended for power. Virtually ignored by the mainstream corporate media, they failed to register much in the national electoral arena. Pérez (1974–1979) was ultimately victorious with over forty-nine percent of the vote. He assumed the presidency at a very promising moment for Venezuela. The Arab-Israeli conflict of 1973—known as

Figure 4 The skyline of Caracas. Urban poor live side by side with modern high rises.

the Yom Kippur War—and the subsequent Arab oil embargo dramatically increased the price of oil from a little over three dollars, where it had been for some time, to well over twelve dollars a barrel, providing a financial bonanza to the new government. Without having to increase production, the government stood to make windfall profits and could now fulfill the promise of using oil to stimulate alternative forms of development (Figure 4).

Pérez's inauguration in 1974 represented only the third peaceful transfer of power to an elected president in Venezuela. On several previous occasions, his party had staked out a position against nationalization: however, in his inaugural speech Pérez addressed his intention to assert state control of foreign oil and steel interests. Early in his government, he established a commission that included government officials, business interests, labor leaders, academics, and the political parties, including those on the left. In typical bombastic style, Pérez promised to implement a broad social and economic agenda that would tackle the recurrent problems of inflation and speculation on basic goods, improve agricultural production, fund an ambitious program of large-scale infrastructure projects that would employ thousands, introduce new labor reforms, and revamp the social security program.

Flush with foreign reserves, the Pérez administration sought to exploit bauxite and aluminum deposits, expand petrochemical production, push forward construction of the Caracas subway, modernize the international airport, and expand hydroelectric output, along with a host of other projects. The state bureaucracy expanded dramatically, adding hundreds of new administrators and bureaucrats to the national budget to oversee these new endeavors. To address Venezuela's lack of trained professionals, the Pérez government established a scholarship program known as the *Mariscal de Ayacucho* that sent hundreds to universities in the United States and Europe. These reforms and others provided the general contours of what Pérez would subsequently call his *Gran Venezuela* project. Assuming the price of oil would continue to increase, Pérez also borrowed from foreign creditors to jump-start his ever-expanding project. Shortly after assuming the presidency, to further promote his ambitious plan he requested and received from Congress special powers to rule by decree and without consulting with the legislature, powers known as *Leyes Habilitantes* (Enabling Laws).

On the international front, Pérez recast Venezuela's foreign relations, proposing a multipolar policy. He lent support to the nonaligned movement; served as an international broker in efforts to oust the dictator of Nicaragua, Anastasio Somoza; and championed Panama's effort to establish control of its canal. Though he remained anticommunist, he also broke with Betancourt and reestablished diplomatic relations with Cuba in 1974. Pérez also established a "Program of Financial Cooperation" to help cash strapped Central American nations obtain oil under less onerous terms.

When did Venezuela nationalize its oil industry?

At the end of 1974, Pérez signed a law that nationalized the steel industry. In dealing with oil, however, Pérez proceeded more cautiously, although the foreign oil companies did not really resist the process of nationalization: they expected that they would be handsomely compensated. Nationalization in Venezuela represented an effort on the part of the state to acquire the assets of the foreign-controlled industry that extracted the nation's petroleum reserves. Venezuela has always retained ownership over its oil; it had never relinquished control of subsoil rights.

The formula by which the foreign companies would receive compensation and the issue of future joint enterprises became points of contention. In addressing compensation, the government selected a generous formula that benefited the foreign oil companies. The matter of joint enterprises drew the greatest attention. Former president Caldera opposed Article 5 of the proposed legislation, insisting that it left open a back door to the nationalization process permitting foreign companies to create joint enterprises and derive profits from those entities while the state assumed all the risks. Pérez Alfonzo, the former Minister of Hydrocarbons under Betancourt and one of the founders of OPEC, derided the legislation, calling it a *"nacionalización chucuta"* (small nationalization). In 1976, Pérez Alfonzo published a collection of essays entitled *Hundiéndonos en el excremento del diablo* (*Sinking in the Excrement of the Devil*) in reference to Venezuela's relation with oil, concluding that after nationalization *"el petróleo es nuestro, lo demás lo importamos"* ("the oil is ours, everything else we import").[2]

The US government actually considered the Venezuelan government's approach to nationalization to be "moderate" since it allowed for contracts with foreign firms after it was enacted. To assuage opposition concerns, former president Betancourt joined the fray and lent his support to joint enterprises. The opposition in the congress was not convinced by

Betancourt's affirmation. The legislation that nationalized the Venezuelan oil industry was approved with only the support of AD and the small *Cruzada Cívica Nacionalista* or CCN (Civic Nationalist Crusade), a party created earlier by Pérez Jiménez supporters. All the other parties—COPEI, MEP, MAS, and PCV—that in principle supported the nationalization of the industry voted against the watered-down AD-sponsored legislation. A victorious Pérez signed the bill into law on August 29, 1975, and it took effect on January 1, 1976.

The oil nationalization legislation did not resolve the issue of foreign participation in the industry. After having fully compensated European and US firms, the petroleum industry, under the newly created holding company *Petróleos de Venezuela* (PdVSA), took control of fourteen different oil firms. To mark the nationalization Pérez visited Mene Grande, site of the first commercially productive well in 1914, and raised the Venezuelan flag over the Zumaque well. The fourteen affiliates of the foreign companies received Venezuelan names and gradually PdVSA absorbed these enterprises. By 1986, only three companies still operated—Lagoven, Maraven, and Corpoven—and by 1997 they were subsumed by PdVSA.

Despite now being formally "Venezuelan," the companies retained the operating culture and structure of their foreign predecessors. The new directors of PdVSA had previously been executives of the foreign companies, and sought to insulate the enterprises from the government, especially oversight by the Ministry of Mines, a trend that intensified in ensuing decades. Critics accused these directors of trying to create a parallel state structure independent of the national government. Just as significantly, the foreign oil companies never fully departed, and foreigners continued to participate as technical advisors, sharing operating programs, and, as predicted, forming joint enterprises with PdVSA. The "back door" part of the nationalization that Pérez had proposed and that Caldera and Pérez Alfonzo feared soon materialized. Heavy crude deposits in the Orinoco basin, where foreign companies operated, were classified as bitumen and charged significantly reduced royalties.

How had oil transformed Venezuela by the 1980s?

From the discovery of the Mene Grande fields in 1914 up to the 1980s, Venezuela had been producing oil for world markets for over sixty years. With thousands of wells, the country produced about three million barrels a day. From 1917 through 1975 it had produced approximately 31.972 million barrels of oil.[3] Lake Maracaibo and the adjoining area contained the highest petroleum reserves in Venezuela. Dependence on oil had increased and it represented the lion's share of exports and the government's principal source of revenue. Despite its importance to the national economy, employment in the oil industry in the 1980s represented less than one percent of the labor force, employing only a little over twenty thousand workers. Oil workers continued to receive the highest wages and benefits among the Venezuelan working class. Employment in the industry increasingly relied on family networks or personal contacts.

Given the country's population was over fifteen million, of which more than seventy percent lived in urban areas, political elites emphasized that the oil industry benefited the country and had transformed the lives of most Venezuelans. They had a point. A significant percentage of the population had slowly experienced an improved standard of living and, as of 1974, Venezuela boasted the highest per capita income in Latin America. However, distribution of income was one of the most lopsided in the continent. According to a study in 1974, while *campesinos*, the rural population, survived on five hundred bolívares a year, professional sectors earned 72,000 bolívares a year, or 144 times what the poor earned.[4] High-rise buildings dominated the urban landscape, elegant nightclubs attracted socialites, and five-star hotels provided accommodations for foreign visitors. The uneven distribution was symbolized by ownership of cars. Old and newer-model Chevrolets, Chryslers, and Fords clogged streets—some of which had been designed for earlier forms of transportation—or the freeways that crisscrossed the narrow Caracas valley.

New subdivisions sprung up in most major cities, modern supermarkets took the place of family stores and local bodegas, and ubiquitous *centros commerciales* (shopping malls) serviced consumers eager to purchase the latest fashion or newest merchandise. Self-serve supermarkets opened new outlets for Venezuelan manufacturers and the mass distribution of consumer goods. Proponents of modernity could proudly assert that most people slept in beds rather than *hamacas* (hammocks) and wore shoes instead of the traditional cloth sandals known as *alpargatas*. Cigarettes replaced rolled *tobacco an chimo* (a mixture of tobacco and *urao* or trona) that was chewed by the lower classes. Wealthier Venezuelans drank imported Scotch whiskey and became among Latin America's highest consumers of beer—largely nationally-produced Polar or Zulia—leaving behind *aguardiente* and *miche,* cheap distilled liquors.

Increased purchasing power allowed wealthier sectors to jet to Miami for the weekend and many wealthy Venezuelans began to purchase property in South Florida. With a relatively strong currency valued at 4,30 bolivares to the dollar, Venezuelans abroad acquired the reputation as the Saudis of Latin America, who when shopping purportedly claimed *"ta barato,"* it's cheap, and *"dame dos,"* give me two of everything. In 1975 Florida exported $562 million dollars in goods to Venezuela; by 1982 it reached $2.3 billion. During the 1970s, Venezuela had its own international airline VIASA, that provided service to the United States and Europe. In 1976, the supersonic Concorde began service, if only briefly, between Paris and Caracas, affirming Venezuela's newfound status as a major oil producer. The cover of *Bohemia* (January 30-February 5, 1978), a popular local weekly magazine, proclaimed that Miami was "being fattened with Venezuelan petrodollars." According to one report, over 250,000 Venezuelans flew to

Miami on shopping sprees during 1981, bringing back clothing, appliances, and other consumer goods. Florida exports to
Venezuela served as a measure of the economic boom.

The boom conditions and the wider diffusion of foreign
consumer values and culture invariably raised concerns about
Venezuelan culture. Foreign films, especially from Hollywood,
dominated the movie theaters; the latest pop music blasted
from radios, and dubbed US television programs competed
with local *telenovelas* (soap operas).

The seeming diminishment of Venezuelan cultural expressions worried some. One government document in the
mid-1970s summarized the dilemma by saying that except for
llanera (plains) music and to a lesser extent *gaitas* music mainly
from Zulia Venezuela lacked a popular musical tradition.
The government lamented that it had nothing with which to
counter the proliferation of Colombian *cumbias* and newer *val-
lenatos* and other musical styles. Subsequent administrations
imposed a one-for-one law, obligating radio stations to play
one Venezuelan song for every foreign tune they played (it
was enforced sporadically and for a short time).

In rural areas, investments by governments in housing,
potable water, electrification, education, and health campaigns
to end malaria and other tropical diseases improved conditions. Life expectancy, which had hovered at thirty-three in
the 1930s, reached fifty-five in the 1950s, and sixty-eight by
the late 1970s. In addition to government programs, disadvantaged groups received some relief from Caritas, a Catholic
charity, and agricultural surplus products from the American-
operated Alliance for Progress. The continued existence of
poverty, evidenced by the presence of the massive shanty-
towns in Caracas and other urban centers, underscored the
persistent problem of inequality confronting Venezuela. Next
to the high-rise towers of Caracas, Valencia, and Maracaibo
were the *ranchos* that singer-songwriter Alí Primera described
in 1974 in what is probably the best known Venezuelan song
in Latin America, *Las casas de cartón* ("Houses of Cardboard").

Gradually, and beginning in the oil-rich 1970s and 1980s, consumerism penetrated even the poorest sectors of society. The makeshift and cardboard structures became permanent edifices as a new generation crafted homes from cement blocks and zinc roofs. Even though many urban residents lacked access to basic services, satellite dishes beamed in television signals, exposing them to a lifestyle largely out of their reach. Urban poor, many operating in the informal sector or as street vendors known as *buhoneros*, pressured city governments and gradually acquired services such as electricity and access to water.

Violent crime continued to be a significant issue in Venezuela in these same decades; typically, the Monday edition of newspapers reported on the number of deaths that occurred on the weekend. Upscale residents learned to live in fear of the day the poor from the hills would descend on the city; crime rates, including murder, continued to be among the highest in Latin America. Many homes of the middle classes and the well-to-do increasingly began to resemble fortresses. The high walls encrusted with sharp multicolor glass shards subsequently gave way to the sophisticated security systems, electrified fences, and armed private guards that we find today.

Those living in poor sectors also took steps to protect themselves, forming local associations to patrol the neighborhood and to keep out gangs and petty drug dealers. In the mid-1960s, concerned with the growing crime rate, government officials attempted to lower the age at which police could charge youths as adults from eighteen to fourteen. Increasingly authorities focused on youths of color from the poorer neighborhoods that encircled urban centers such as Caracas. The association between youths of color and crime continued to dominate much of the discourse on crime in contemporary Venezuela. As long as violence was contained to the poor hillside barrios, government officials could dismiss it as the product of social deviance or as an aberration from an otherwise orderly society. Even so, these conditions served as a constant reminder that sharp economic and even racial inequalities coexisted in the shadow of the modern oil economy.

As the Pérez administration neared the end of its term in 1979, it became clear that the huge economic bonanza had done little to reduce the pronounced social and class differences. Moreover, charges of favoritism, inefficiency, and corruption shadowed most of Pérez's four years in office. One of the most blatant examples under Pérez involved the purchase of an older and malfunctioning cold-storage ship renamed the *Sierra Nevada*, for which the government paid several million dollars over its real value. The *Sierra Nevada* case exposed how government officials and their allies used the national treasury to enrich themselves. Serving as intermediaries in the purchase of the vessel, government officials charged exorbitant commissions for their purported services, thus inflating the price of the ship. A congressional investigation over the *Sierra Nevada* fell a few votes short of finding Pérez guilty of malfeasance and moral turpitude. A guilty verdict would have prohibited him from ever seeking a new term as president.

Pérez's personal dalliance became the subject of public conversation, as he maintained a relatively open relationship with Cecilia Matos, his personal secretary. Matos exercised significant power in the Pérez administration, serving as an intermediary for those who sought access to the president. Upon Pérez's death in 2011—years after he had left office, but continued to be an influential figure—the dispute between his wife, Blanca Rodríguez, and Matos, with whom he had lived in Miami, erupted into the open as both sought control of his body and disputed whether he should be buried in Florida or in Venezuela. After a nine-month legal battle, during which Pérez's body remained in cold storage, he was eventually buried in Caracas.

What was the legacy of nationalization and the Gran Venezuela Project after 1978?

Dissatisfaction with the Pérez administration became evident in the final years of his administration. COPEI's candidate Luis

Herrera Campins tapped into this discontent and won the presidential elections in 1978. As in previous elections, support for left candidates José Vicente Rangel and Luis Beltrán Prieto Figueroa remained in single digits. In the wake of Pérez's free spending policies, Herrera (1979–1984) faced a country with depleted coffers and a mounting foreign debt. Portending a new attitude, in a *New York Times* interview Herrera insisted, "Venezuela should aspire to be known as a land of work, sacrifice, and discipline, instead of a guzzler of whiskey and oil." Efforts by the government to prevent television stations from transmitting whiskey and cigarette advertisements were met with skepticism, and in some circles ridicule.

Herrera's government inherited many of the unfinished mega-projects initiated by the former president that continued to sap the treasury, but the president feared the political repercussions of stopping projects in mid-construction and dismissing thousands of workers and bureaucrats. The Venezuelan economy began to decelerate, as access to credit tightened and internal production decreased, fueling unemployment. While still borrowing to fund projects, the government reduced expenditures in other areas, eliminated price controls, and eased restrictions on imports to compensate for decreased production. In the wake of the Iranian revolution (1979) and the subsequent war between Iran and Iraq (1980–1988) the price of oil increased, creating a second boom. This price increase temporarily masked economic problems, and the Herrera administration continued to borrow short-term high-interest loans from foreign banks. Under Herrera the size of the state continued to grow; public employees reached 1.1 million, representing according to one source "one out of every four workers" in Venezuela.[5] The price of goods began to skyrocket, and inflation reached new levels.

By 1982 the price of oil had decreased and Venezuela once again faced a downturn exacerbated now by a growing debt crisis. Foreign debt, which had been eleven billion dollars in 1978 under Pérez, reached twenty-seven billion dollars under Herrera by 1983, and by 1984 it had expanded to thirty-four billion. Several studies stressed that wasteful planning and corruption, including contracts to phantom companies under Pérez and Herrera, contributed to the sky-rocketing debt. Venezuelans with access to liquid capital converted their weaker currency to dollars, fueling capital flight. Nationalization of the oil industry was, in fact, not accompanied by the so-called sowing of profits and did nothing to decrease dependence on petroleum or protect the country from fluctuating oil prices.

Pressure on the overvalued currency, which for twenty years had been pegged at 4.3 to the dollar, increased. On Friday February 18, 1983, the government announced the devaluation of the bolivar and established a multitier system that controlled the price of essential items while allowing the bolivar to float for nonessential items. On the unregulated market, the bolivar climbed to 13 to the dollar. Currency speculation became rampant. While it established a new policy, the government suspended the sale of dollars. Popularly known as *viernes negro* (Black Friday) in echo of Wall Street's Great Crash, the devaluation dashed popular perceptions, especially among the middle classes, that oil would protect Venezuelans from the economic crisis that had begun to engulf most of Latin America. As many Venezuelans saw their savings erode, the Herrera government had to fend off accusations that it had counseled close allies about the impending devaluation and allowed them to convert their funds to dollars. Before the imposition of controls, the *New York Times* reported that during mid-February alone over 200 million dollars a day left the country. *El Nacional*, a leading national newspaper, subsequently published an account estimating that billions of dollars had left the country before the devaluation.

For many Venezuelans, devaluation represented a watershed moment—"the end of the fiesta" as many referred to it, a precursor of future devaluations, diminishing purchasing power, increased corruption, and the future crisis that would grip the country. Some who had bought real estate in Florida and expected the exchange rate to remain stable found it impossible to make payments. Eventually the government established a formal agency, the Office of Differential Exchange, known as *Recadi*, to oversee access to dollars. It quickly became mired in controversy and charges of favoritism and corruption. As discontent increased, the government clamped down on some critics, and public reproach increasingly targeted both parties and the *Punto Fijo* accords established in 1958. The rise of neighborhood associations among poorer sectors and civic organizations among middle classes not associated with the traditional parties underscored that important elements of the population had begun to lose faith in the political system.

In the final years of his administration, Herrera, who had initially sided with Washington on most foreign policy matters, departed from his prior position by supporting Argentina against England in the Malvinas/Falklands war. Venezuela became one of the only countries to support Argentina openly. To express his displeasure with the British, Herrera prohibited Scotch from being served at official government functions, forcing, according to one newspaper, functionaries to hide their bottles in paper bags. He also supported a proposal by Mexico and France that sought a negotiated solution to the US intervention in the war in El Salvador.

Did a shift in government alleviate the crisis?

As Venezuelans reeled from the economic crisis, they faced a new presidential election in December of 1983 that pitted former President Caldera of COPEI against the nominee of AD, Jaime Lusinchi, a former pediatrician, as well as two left-wing candidates. Unsurprisingly, Lusinchi won the elections by fifty-six percent, to a distant thirty-four percent for Caldera, who was running for a fifth time and could not distance himself from Herrera's handling of the economy. Despite worsening economic conditions, the two leftist candidates, the perennial José Vicente Rangel and Teodoro Petkoff, founder and leader of the MAS, together received seven percent of the vote.

Under pressure to address the volatile economic situation, Lusinchi (1984–1989) began to implement a general package of austerity measures that bore a resemblance to prescriptions proposed by the International Monetary Fund (IMF). Without questioning the legality of the debt, he temporarily refinanced a portion of the short-term obligations acquired under Herrera and reduced public expenditures and salaries. As a result, growth declined precipitously and unemployment reached a record eleven percent. Like many of his predecessors, Lusinchi requested and received authority to govern by decree (*Leyes Habilitantes*).

In 1986, the government purchased interest in CITGO; the acquisition was completed in 1990, giving *Petróleos de Venezuela* access to refining and distribution networks in the United States. For the directors of PdVSA, the purchase of CITGO served to position the company as an international oil conglomerate. Critics contended that CITGO's refineries were not suited to process Venezuela's heavier crude products. The policy of acquiring foreign assets, in practice internationalizing PdVSA, allowed the holding company to hide profits from the government; their having purchased many of these assets at inflated prices also provided a disincentive against their sale by any future government.

The deterioration of the economy became evident in the continued decline of the bolivar to the dollar from 15 in 1985 to 25 in 1986. Inflation spiraled upward, reaching twenty-five percent in 1988. Increasingly, the government used reserves to cover the deficit, temporarily stabilizing conditions. The emergence of several Venezuelan-produced brands of Scotch, according to the *Wall Street Journal*, served as an indicator that the country had "fallen on hard times": by contrast, in 1978, the country had imported 26.4 million bottles of Scotch, affirming its role as one of the largest per capita consumers in the world.

Lusinchi soon became mired in various scandals; one involved his open relationship with his personal secretary, Blanca Ibáñez, who, according to the opposition, approved cabinet appointments and even the promotion and removal of generals. The public spectacle surrounding Lusinchi and Ibáñez, including the extramarital affair, charges of corruption, influence peddling, criticisms from the Church, and intrigue, mirrored the steamy *telenovelas* that Venezuelans faithfully watched on nightly prime time television. On multiple occasions Ibáñez was accused of authorizing contracts without competition, influence peddling, and the purchase of homes and cars with public funds.

When Lusinchi awarded Blanca Ibáñez the "Order of the Liberator," the highest honor issued to a civilian, some legislators demanded an investigation. In a largely male-dominated political world, there is no doubt that her position as a woman, and a Colombian, made her a tempting target in the climate of corruption that pervaded the Lusinchi government. The fact that one male opposition politician, also tainted by charges, could insist that Ibáñez had become "the symbol of modern day corruption" bears this out. The public spectacle that surrounded Lusinchi and Ibáñez plagued most of his administration and on several occasions the government moved to muzzle the press and restrict criticisms.

Several other matters surfaced that evidenced the increasing climate of repression as well as the impunity that police and military authorities enjoyed during the Lusinchi administration. In May 1986 the *Dirección Nacional de los Servicios de Inteligencia y Prevención* executed nine unarmed members of *Punto Cero*, an insurgent group, in what became known as the Yumare Massacre. After shooting the members, authorities made a point of dressing them in uniforms to validate their claim of self-defense. In 2011 a Venezuelan court found former general Alexis Ramón Sánchez guilty and sentenced him to thirteen years in prison for the murders.

In Petare, the largest collection of poor neighborhoods in eastern Caracas, police repeatedly cracked down on barrio residents who protested deteriorating economic conditions. Catholic clergy who worked among the poor placed advertisements in several Caracas newspapers accusing the police of perpetrating "brutal, arbitrary and aggressive actions." Despite widespread support, including from Catholic authorities, to most people's surprise the government insisted that protests by Petare residents represented a broader subversive campaign to destabilize the government.

Another incident in 1988 involved the shooting of fourteen fishermen in the state of Apure by military authorities that sought to portray them as guerrillas. Lusinchi offered a press conference supporting the military's version of events. Occurring as the presidential campaign for Lusinchi's successor unfolded, the issue acquired national importance and even Acción Democrática officials distanced themselves from the president. The existence of two survivors served to contradict the official version of events; the government eventually compensated the victims' families.

Recadi, the Office of Differential Exchange, charged with currency control and founded under Herrera, had generated charges of corruption since its inception, but under Lusinchi the accusations intensified. Inquiries by Movimiento al Socialismo legislators and by journalists documented the climate of favoritism that existed under both Herrera and Lusinchi, including requests for dollars at preferential rates for ministers, governors, army officials, and political allies. Dollars received at preferential rates and sold on the free market generated sizable profits. In some cases, real and phantom companies used government connections to acquire dollars for nonexistent purchases. During its existence, Recadi transacted billions of dollars yet failed to keep adequate records of its transactions. The lack of oversight and outright corruption in the various agencies charged with providing subsidized dollars continued to be a recurring problem.

The other matter involving Lusinchi that surfaced after the administration ended involved the purchase of sixty-five Jeeps purportedly bought for use by police and security forces, but which instead went to AD officials as they prepared for the presidential elections. On this matter the Supreme Court ruled that evidence existed to proceed to trial and removed Lusinchi's immunity, although after several efforts nothing occurred, since by that point the ex-president had left the country and was living in Miami. Likewise, in 1991, after she had formally married Lusinchi, a Venezuelan court absolved Blanca Ibáñez of all corruption charges, even though evidence surfaced of a Florida bank account with over six million dollars, reinforcing for many the climate of impunity that the wealthy political class of both parties enjoyed in Venezuela.

What was the Caracazo and how did it influence Venezuelan politics?

The *Caracazo* refers to a massive popular rebellion that rocked Venezuela in February of 1989, fueled by government efforts to impose economic austerity measures. The protest highlighted the growing social discontent and the contradictions evident in the political system under which the country had been governed since 1958. The event became a watershed in Venezuelan politics, recasting alliances and energizing new social movements.

As the campaign for the presidency unfolded in 1988, full-page advertisements in major national newspapers featured former president Luis Herrera and Comité de Organización Política Electoral Independiente's candidate for the presidency, Eduardo Fernández, embracing against a stark black background. The symbolism was not lost on Venezuelans who had seen their savings slashed on the so-called "Black Friday" when the currency had been devalued in February

1983. The ads blamed COPEI and its leaders for not only deval-
uing the national currency, but also for having devalued the
country, conflating nationalism with the value of the currency.
This equation rested on the assumption that oil would protect
Venezuela from the crisis that other Latin American nations
experienced.

Against this backdrop, new elections in December of 1988
returned to power the charismatic Carlos Andres Pérez of
Acción Democrática with fifty-two percent of the vote, defeating Eduardo Fernández of COPEI, who garnered forty percent. As had occurred in all the previous elections since 1958,
the leftist candidate Teodoro Petkoff of the Movimiento al
Socialismo received less than three percent of the vote. In the
weeks before the inauguration Pérez (1989–1993) embarked on
a world tour that took him to South America, the Middle East,
and Europe, where he criticized the onerous foreign debt that
saddled most countries in Latin America. Yet critics likened
Pérez's lavish and costly inauguration ceremonies in 1989 to
a coronation. As a testament to his reputation on the international stage, over twenty-four world leaders attended the
inauguration, including Spain's Felipe González, Cuba's Fidel
Castro, US Vice President Dan Quayle, and Nicaragua's Daniel
Ortega.

As an oil producer, Venezuela had generally avoided the
severe austerity measures that the IMF and the World Bank
had imposed on other governments in the aftermath of the
debt crisis that gripped Latin America during the 1980s.
Venezuela's wealthy had grown accustomed to believing that
the oil economy would protect their standard of living and
that they lived in an "exceptional" nation. Although working and poorer sectors of society had failed to benefit equally
from oil wealth, they nonetheless anticipated certain benefits,
including food subsidies, cheap transportation, and access to
education. Pérez, who had campaigned promising a return to
"good times" and opposition to neoliberal austerity policies,
did an about-face once in office. Although publicly critical of

the onerous foreign debt that Latin America faced, he rejected a moratorium on the thirty-four billion dollars Venezuela owned foreign banks. He took no measures to address capital flight from Venezuela, an amount that almost equaled the foreign debt.

On February 16, 1989, Pérez outlined the government's plan. Following a recipe of austerity measures typically mandated by the IMF that placed the burden on those sectors least able to afford such measures, he authorized a one hundred percent increase in the price of gasoline, with associated increases in public transportation; put an end to subsidies on food (except for a few hard to find basic products); increased the price of most services including electricity, water, telephone, and natural gas, and floated the currency. The government anticipated that the *paquetazo* (the package), as the measures became known, would increase inflation by forty percent, but had not foreseen that it would generate significant public outcry.

On Monday morning February 27, to compensate for the increase in the price of gasoline, bus and car drivers began to charge in excess of the new thirty percent price set by the government. Commuters who made the daily trek into Caracas for work and students who had long enjoyed special subsidized rates became the flashpoint of the public discontent. At the *Nuevo Circo*, the city's central transportation hub, student protests spread, shutting down adjacent avenues and eventually the main freeways. University students and thousands of couriers on motorbike also joined in. Dissatisfaction quickly spread throughout working-class neighborhoods where people set up barricades, burned tires, and attacked cars and buses. Thousands joined the protests in Caracas. Overwhelmed, the metropolitan police stood powerless, or, in some cases joined the angry crowds as they targeted supermarkets and shopping centers and carted off everything from food to appliances and furniture. The events that transpired in Caracas also played out in other Venezuelan cities.

Even as protests engulfed Caracas and other cities, Pérez did not appear to comprehend the magnitude of what his government faced. Unperturbed, he travelled to Barquisimeto in the state of Lara and addressed a meeting of Venezuelan executives. Eventually, the government mobilized the armed forces, mostly young recruits from the interior of the country, to restore order. Before announcing the suspension of civil liberties and declaring a state of siege on national television, Pérez met with party and opposition leaders in Miraflores (the Venezuelan presidential palace).

The situation only worsened. Ordered to patrol the streets, the military shot scores of protesters. Caracas's principal morgue, at Bello Monte, announced it could not accommodate more bodies. Unable to find their relatives, hundreds of frantic citizens descended on the morgue and searched the impromptu list of the deceased placed on walls. The number of those killed has never been completely established, and estimates range from a few hundred to several thousand. In the interior, authorities gained the upper hand while in Caracas isolated protests continued until March 4.

The Caracazo, as the events became known, sent shock waves throughout the political establishment in Venezuela and had repercussions that were felt in Washington as well. The violent protest revealed the extent to which most Venezuelans had lost faith in the parties and political institutions, and instead lashed out at commercial symbols in their midst. The government's incapacity to foresee problems in the wake of their austerity measures underscores the extent to which they had lost touch with the conditions in the country.

Traditional assumptions about the nature of an ordered society that had ameliorated class and racial difference and the viability of its democracy had been shaken. Amid the soul-searching that ensued, Venezuelans faced a new national reality. The dominant narrative, the product of the Punto Fijo accords, no longer held sway over significant numbers of citizens. Some observers recognized that Venezuela would never be the same. One historian lamented that he thought he had understood Venezuela yet it took only three days for his understanding to come undone.[6]

While it reestablished order, the Pérez government temporarily rescinded some of the most draconian measures that had evoked the public outcry. Despite continued opposition, including strikes, the government proceeded with the application of austerity measures, including the wholesale privatization of former state enterprises, ending price controls on consumer items, and allowing foreign capital a freer hand in the economy. In 1991 the government authorized the sale of the airline VIASA to the Spanish carrier Iberia, itself on the verge of bankruptcy.

Employing an argument repeated throughout Latin America, proponents of privatization and the introduction of foreign capital insisted that private business would streamline enterprises, modernize installations, expand choice, and provide better services. These claims underplayed the fact that wherever it was applied, privatization usually brought a reduction of the workforce, a dismantling of union contracts to lower wages, and eventually a rise in prices to the consumer, all boosting the profits of mostly foreign owners. The dismissal of public and private employees swelled the ranks of the informal economy of a form that inflation reduced people's purchasing power. By the end of 1991 with inflation skyrocketing, poverty increased dramatically.

Violence increased noticeably during the 1990s. Deaths from gunshots swelled, according to one newspaper, to over two hundred killings a month. One opinion poll rated crime as the number one concern, displacing the economy and unemployment. Fears over security increased, benefiting private firms that offered guards, electronic surveillance, and even personal bodyguards. In upper-class neighborhoods, the ubiquitous figure of a guard perched on a stool in front of a house holding a sawed-off shotgun became common. Kidnappings, usually associated with the unsafe border region, especially with Colombia, spread to the city, and the phenomenon known as *secuestro express* (express kidnappings), where a person is abducted for several hours while their ATM account is depleted, began to generate fear among wealthier sectors.

What motivated the coups of 1992?

On the early morning of February 4, 1992, residents of Caracas awoke to the sound of repeated automatic and small arms gunfire. Military coups, especially those that gripped Latin America during the late 1970s, had traditionally been motivated by right-wing interests and sought to protect the privileges of the wealthier classes. But these rebels, claiming to represent the forces of the *Movimiento Bolivariano Revolucionario 200* or MBR 200 (Revolutionary Bolivarian Movement 200), suggested a different agenda. In addition, assertions from this group concerning the unfinished work of liberator Simón Bolívar and his mentor Simón Rodríguez distinguished them from right-wing military forces.

As the events unfolded, it became clear that mid-level army officers, commanders of armored divisions, and paratroopers had attempted to capture President Pérez, place him on trial for corruption, install a civilian/military government, and call for a new constitutional convention. Their plan faced problems from the beginning: rumors circulated about a possible rebellion and authorities took measures to protect the president. Returning from a trip to Davos, Switzerland where he had met with business groups, Pérez first went to La Casona, his residence, where he managed to elude capture. Pérez then drove to Miraflores, the presidential palace, where he again confronted a rebel. Using a tunnel beneath the presidential palace he made it to a television station, from where he addressed the nation, rallied loyal forces in the military, and called for civilian support.

The capture of Pérez had been central to the insurgents' plans, as he was the unpopular advocate of neoliberal policies that had produced the outcry on February 1989. The plan also included seizing several military installations throughout the city and broadcasting an address to the nation. Rebels managed to detain high-ranking officers and neutralize opposition in Valencia, Maracay, and Maracaibo. Insurgents also had support at garrisons in Mérida, Táchira, and several other states. Led by a young lieutenant coronel named Hugo Rafael Chávez Frías, who had been assigned to the Miraflores operation, a contingent of rebel forces remained at the nearby Military Museum after they had failed to control the presidential palace. Without the capture of the presidential palace and with Pérez transmitting on television, support from other military units in Caracas did not materialize and the plan began to unravel.

Facing difficult odds and wanting to avoid further bloodshed, Chávez conceded defeat and surrendered by noon on February 4th. Confronting mutinous troops in Maracay, authorities allowed Chávez to speak to the media and appeal for them to surrender. Proclaiming to lead a Bolivarian movement, Chávez assumed full responsibility for the failure of operations in Caracas, called on his colleagues to surrender and asserted that *por ahora* ("for now") the rebels had failed to achieve their objectives. In a society in which people had endured repeated corruption scandals and in which politicians seldom assumed responsibility for their actions, the statement captivated people and thrust Chávez onto the national stage. After their arrest, authorities confined the leaders of the rebellion to the San Carlos detention center in Caracas, the same building that had housed guerrillas during the 1960s.

Who was Hugo Rafael Chávez Frias?

Born in 1954, in Sabaneta in the plains state of Barinas, Hugo Chávez soon emerged as the leader of the anti-establishment movement. His background as a rural mixed-race Venezuelan made him capable of talking to people in a folksy way that reflected their own experiences. As rural public teachers with seven children, Chávez's parents were quite poor. For a time, Chávez and his elder brother Adan had to live with their grandmother. After completing secondary school, where he honed his skills as a baseball player for the Barinas state team, Chávez applied for entrance to the military academy in 1971. Having initially failed the chemistry entrance exam, his performance on the baseball field eventually assured his admission into the academy. More importantly, the military offered an opportunity for social mobility traditionally inaccessible to someone from Chávez's socioeconomic background.

The revolt by colonel Hugo Trejo in 1958 and the subsequent experiences throughout the 1960s reflected the existence of an important left-wing tendency within the Venezuelan military. By the early 1970s, the armed forces underwent an important change, offering not only traditional military training, but also access to a university-level curriculum that exposed students to multiple disciplines, including political economy, philosophy, and history. While at the academy, the officers could also attend classes at the national university, where they engaged with other students and debated radical ideas. Rather than a class apart, increasingly the military reflected the social and political tensions evident in society. For his part, Chávez read broadly, drew inspiration from Venezuelan history, and began to see the army as a potential agent of social change.

After graduation, Chávez was assigned to a counterinsurgency squadron in his home state, although he did not see any combat against what remained of the small leftist guerrilla movement. Future assignments took him throughout the country where he encountered like-minded officers and soldiers concerned about the political direction of the country, repeated cases of corruption, and alleviating the increasing rate of poverty. At age twenty-three he met and eventually married Nancy Colmenares, his first wife, with whom he had three children. In 1977 Chávez formed an insurgent group within the military known as the *Ejercito de Liberación del*

Pueblo de Venezuela or ELPV (Venezuelan's People Liberation Army) and began to expand contacts with progressive political figures.

In 1981, after having attained the rank of captain, Chávez became an instructor at the military academy in Caracas, where he shared his evolving notions of a "Bolivarian ideal" with the young cadets. Military authorities began to track his moves and expressed concern about his actions. To commemorate Bolívar's death, in 1982, at the base in Maracay, Chávez gave a speech on the contemporary importance of the Liberator's legacy to the country. Subsequently, Chávez and several fellow officers took an oath and formed the *Ejército Bolivariano Revolucionario-200* (Bolivarian Revolutionary Army-200), and then sought to recruit others to join their still vaguely defined cause. The EBR-200 became the impetus for the future *Movimiento Bolivariano Revolucionario 200* or MBR 200 (Bolivarian Revolutionary Movement 200) that brought together military and civilians concerned over the direction of the country.

The 1989 Caracazo and the government's use of the military to repress the civilian population became an important turning point for the young rebels in drawing recruits to their cause. Assigned to eastern Venezuela, and largely isolated, despite outreach with civilians, the movement had been floundering. In much the same way as it fractured the Punto Fijo Pact, the Caracazo splintered the military and created the conditions for the coup of 1992.

On November 27, 1992, as Chávez and his colleagues sat in the cells in the San Carlos Presidio, the sound of airplanes over Caracas signaled a new attempted coup. Civilian collaborators commandeered the public television station and transmitted a poorly made video, smuggled out of the garrison, of Chávez urging Venezuelans to revolt. Led by senior military officers, including elements of the air force and navy, rebels took La Libertador air base in Maracay and contested for control of La Carlota, the air force base in the center of Caracas. Civilians in several cities expressed their support by beating pots and pans and displaying flags, while others protested in the streets and clashed with authorities. In the end, coup leaders failed to capture Pérez or free Chávez from prison and form an interim civilian/military government. Some of the coup plotters escaped by plane to Peru where the government granted them exile. Though Pérez survived another coup, his authority and prestige suffered another severe blow.

Calls for Pérez's resignation increased among diverse circles even after his government had restored order. By March 1993 the attorney general reopened a case over the embezzlement of seventeen million dollars from a *partida secreta* (secret fund), purportedly used for Pérez's lavish inauguration and to provide security for the President of Nicaragua, Violeta Chamorro. Pérez was impeached as president shortly thereafter in an attempt to remove an unpopular political figure whose presence in power jeopardized continued support for Venezuela's frayed political system. Under normal circumstances it is doubtful that the case of the *partida secreta* would have been sufficient motive to impeach Pérez. After some negotiations, Ramón J. Velásquez (1993–1994), a respected historian and a long time member of AD, became interim president.

How did the Venezuelan government try to recuperate from two failed coups?

In the aftermath of the coup of February 1992, discordant voices could be heard in the Congress. Recalling the events of the Caracazo, some political figures proved unwilling to grant Pérez free rein to suspend civil liberties and allow the state to use the coup as a pretext to repress government critics. While he condemned the coup, former president Caldera also criticized policies that undermined people's faith in democracy. Communist Party Congressman Ricardo Gutiérrez reminded his colleagues of how Pérez had turned a deaf ear to popular demands against the economic measures. Others, such as

Congressman Aristóbulo Istúriz of the leftist *Causa R* (Radical Cause) Party, called on the assembly to assess the factors that fomented the coup and popular support for the events. Initially the result of a split with the Communist Party in 1970s, the Causa R drew strength in the 1980s from its emphasis on workers. It led a powerful insurgent union movement in the state of Bolivar, and its candidate became governor there.

Capitalizing on the shifting political tides, Caldera broke from his party and formed *Convergencia* (1993), a new electoral movement. He criticized the Pérez economic package and drew left and center-left support for the elections of December 1993. A collection of smaller left parties popularly referred to as *el chiripero* (swarm of roaches) including *Movimiento al Socialismo, Movimiento Electoral del Pueblo, Unión Republicana Democrática,* and *Partido Comunista de Venezuela* supported Caldera. From its inception Caldera's candidacy sought to tap independent voters not willing to vote for Acción Democrática and Comité de Organización Política Electoral Independiente, but also unlikely to vote for alternative leftist parties. Increasingly associated with the crisis, AD and COPEI experienced a loss of legitimacy and popular support. For its part, AD nominated Claudio Fermin, the previous mayor of the central Caracas Libertador district, and COPEI designated Oswaldo Álvarez Páez, a former governor of the state of Zulia. These candidates not only refused to break with the Pérez-era economic agenda, but spoke of the need to expand the so-called reforms and promote free trade agreements with the United States. The Causa R promoted Andrés Velásquez, its popular labor leader and one-time governor of the state of Bolívar.

With a significant decline in turnout underscoring the growing disenchantment with traditional Venezuelan politics, the four candidates split the vote. Caldera won the elections with thirty-one percent of the vote; the other candidates received a little over twenty percent each. AD and COPEI, the two parties that had dominated Venezuelan political life since 1958, amassed less than fifty percent of the vote. The

twenty-one percent received by Velásquez represented a significant electoral breakthrough for the left; historically its level
of support, among all candidates, had never surpassed ten
percent. If the Caracazo evidenced the failure of the Punto Fijo
agreement, the election of Caldera (1994–1999), one of its archi-
tects, by a coalition of forces that included the left, highlighted
its demise.

Reflecting the support of left-wing parties in his election and needing their vote in the congress, Caldera named
Teodoro Petkoff and Pompeyo Márquez, leading members of
MAS, to his cabinet, the first in finance and the latter to oversee border issues. Another MAS member, Carlos Tablante,
assumed the role of drug czar and quickly became enmeshed
in a series of controversies. In March 1994, Caldera, as he had
done with leftist guerrillas in the 1970s, freed Chávez and his
associates from jail. Out of the military, Chávez and his supporters, including new civilian groups, set out to build his
MBR movement into a national political force.

The Caldera government had promised to chart a new
course, yet even before Caldera assumed the presidency the
banking industry, deregulated under Pérez, experienced a
major crisis. When depositors demanded their money, the
Banco Latino, the second largest in the country, shut its doors.
This further heightened tensions in an already pervasive climate of uncertainty, and with little faith in the government,
account holders demanded access to their funds at other
banks, which also quickly collapsed. The banks that collapsed
represented upward of sixty percent of deposits. Adding to the
growing crisis, many insurance companies proved insolvent,
leaving clients without coverage. A combination of mismanagement and corruption at a time when deregulation provided little oversight produced catastrophic results. Protests
by depositors, in particular pensioners, outside of bank and
government offices became a daily scene.

The government moved to rescue the banks, transferring
public funds to private hands, but this did little to resolve the

crisis. Capital flight increased, including funds the government needed to rescue the banks. As had its predecessors, the Caldera government suspended constitutional guarantees, claiming it needed special powers to deal with the crisis. It increased state oversight of the economy and, claiming it would control speculation, imposed control over foreign exchange and price regulations on basic items. Interest on credit hovered at sixty percent, and by the end of 1994 inflation reached seventy percent. Conditions deteriorated to such an extent that during 1994 close to fifty percent of the population lived in poverty, while over twenty-one percent lived in a situation of abject poverty. Official unemployment reached nearly twenty percent by 1995, and the informal economy provided employment for nearly fifty percent of those seeking employment. As health conditions deteriorated, tropical diseases such as dengue, once curtailed in the 1950s, also reappeared.

No banker responsible for the collapse of banks, illicit enrichment, or other crimes was ever indicted. Some fifty bankers, including Fernando Araujo, Caldera's son-in-law, fled to Miami. Caldera faced mounting criticism, including from Hugo Chávez, who had reentered the political arena, and other critics, who accused the president of nepotism and corruption. Caldera's two sons, son-in-law, and close personal friends all held high government positions in his administration. By 1995, Caldera's popularity plummeted from seventy-eight percent to thirty-one percent.

Although he had promised not to impose IMF-style austerity measures, in April 1996 Caldera introduced his *Agenda Venezuela*, which for many mirrored the earlier Pérez economic package. Fearing another Caracazo, military and police forces were put on alert, as Caldera announced a one hundred percent increase in the price of gasoline and floated the currency, which shot up from 290 to 474 bolivars to the dollar, affecting the price of imported goods. The cost of basic services such as water and electricity also increased, as did a sales tax that now reached 16.5 percent. In an ironic turn of events, Venezuela's negotiator with the IMF had been a former leftist, Teodoro Petkoff, who as director of the Central Office of Coordination and Planning now insisted on the need to "tighten the screws on the Venezuelans." The MAS's association with the Caldera government and the application of neoliberal policies served to delegitimize the party and it lost popular support.

Another area that the Caldera government pursued became known as the *Apertura Petrolera*, or the new Oil Opening. Begun slowly in 1986, a decade after nationalization, the Apertura allowed foreign interests to acquire new concessions. Framed as an effort to use new technology to reactivate previously abandoned oil fields, explore gas reserves off the coast, and tap coal deposits, by the 1990s Petroleos de Venezuela, (the national oil company) began to enter into mixed contracts with foreign and even Venezuelan investors. Lured by low royalties, in some cases lower than those applied by Gómez sixty years earlier, contracts for exploration and development of the Orinoco heavy crude deposits also attracted significant foreign interests.

As this process evolved, PdVSA sought greater independence from the Ministry of Mines, purportedly in order to insulate the company from the volatile political situation the nation confronted. Its leader purposely talked about avoiding the politicization of PdVSA while creating an "internal Maginot line" intended to keep political interests at bay. In reality they sought greater control and less oversight over a process that could potentially generate billions of dollars. With the crisis as the backdrop, representatives from more than one hundred US, European, and Asian corporations filled five-star hotels in Caracas to bid on the new PdVSA concessions. Some sectors predicted that Venezuela would soon experience a new oil bonanza. Critics feared that PdVSA's leaders sought to reverse the earlier nationalization and gradually privatize the company.

The measures adopted by Caldera did little to alleviate the mood of uncertainty and crisis. Moreover, Caldera's prolonged absences from the public stage added to the air of unease. On one occasion in 1997, he even took to the airwaves to contradict a purported astrologist that had predicted his death. Many began to speculate that Caldera's son had become the de facto president.

The economic measures adopted by Caldera had an impact on broad segments of society. During the last two years of his administration, marches, protests, and rallies occurred with frequent regularity. Workers dismissed from the privatized firms, including the national airline VIASA, took to the streets. Others, including university doctors, professors, teachers, students, and workers. mobilized against the Caldera government. Rumors of either potential disorder or impending coups generated yet further uncertainty, and retailers reacted to unsubstantiated claims by closing their *santamarias* (Holy Marys), the popular name given to the rolling metal security doors that covered the entrances to their establishments. With presidential elections scheduled for December 6, 1998, leading political actors and parties began jockeying for position seeking to tap into the growing discontent.

Notes

1. Alexis Blanco, "Interview Pérez Jiménez," *Diario Panorama*, November 9 and 13, 1988.

2. Juan Pablo Pérez Alfonzo, *Hundiéndonos en el excremento del diablo*, Caracas, VZ: Banco Central de Venezuela, 2011, p. 44.

3. Ibid., p. 42.

4. Ibid., p. 43.

5. Juan Tamayo, "Venezuela Suffers Pains of a Petro Junkie," *Miami Herald*, August 23, 1982.

6. Elías Pino Iturrieta, "Un país mas cierto y mas dramático," in *El estallido de febrero,* ed. José Agustín Catalá (Caracas, VZ: Ediciones Centauro, 1989), 11–14.

Part Three

OIL AND REVOLUTION: THE RISE OF HUGO CHÁVEZ

How did Chávez, a former coup leader, win the 1998 presidential election?

During the 1990s, the political landscape in Venezuela shifted as important segments of society, across the entire socioeconomic spectrum, lost faith in the traditional political parties and their ability to reform. Recurring charges of corruption, administrative incompetence, and support for unpopular austerity measures undermined support for traditional parties such as AD and COPEI. For the MAS, participation in the Caldera government and allegations of corruption against its own members called into question the party's ability to represent itself as an alternative political force. Even before the presidential elections of 1998 started, it became apparent they would be different from others held since 1958.

Community organizations, in some cases active since the 1960s, increasingly assumed a greater role in society. In working-class and poor neighborhoods with little or no protection, residents organized and began to police themselves, and even oversaw the delivery of services. Networks formed by Afro-Venezuelans publicly promoted their socioeconomic and cultural contributions to the country, while offering a different narrative of history that challenged prevailing notions of Venezuela as a racial democracy. Indigenous groups erupted onto the national stage, holding protests in Caracas against government efforts to turn over large swaths of territory to mining and logging concerns in the Imataca reserve in the Venezuelan rainforest and elsewhere. In the informal sector, *buhoneros* (street vendors) demanded fair treatment and often clashed with authorities seeking to dislodge them from public spaces. Facing diminished access to education, students from lower socioeconomic groups demanded entry into public universities that had increasingly become dominated by the middle and upper classes. Although organizing by women reflected some of the historic tensions between predominantly middle class feminists and more grassroots demands, their combined efforts highlighted the centrality of women's issues in the political debate, particularly around issues of poverty and inequality.

A poll taken in December of 1997 indicated that 53.4 percent of the population did not favor any of the potential candidates. Reflecting the distrust of formal parties, most candidates vying for the presidency in 1998 purported to be "independents." From the beginning of the year, a new candidate, initially not associated with any political party, began to draw significant attention. As mayor of Chacao, a district of Caracas, Irene Sáez Conde, a former winner of Miss Venezuela and Miss Universe (1981), appeared to lead in popular opinion polls. One of the five municipalities that comprise greater Caracas, Chacao included European immigrant communities and more wealthy sectors such as Altamira, La Castellana, and Los Palos Grandes, as well as the exclusive Country Club area with its eighteen-hole golf course. Nevertheless, amid this affluence, the presence of a poor neighborhood in Chacao, Los Pajaritos (Little Birds), served as a constant reminder of Venezuela's persistent inequality.

As the mayor of Chacao with access to resources, Sáez streamlined the municipal administration, improved the delivery of services, and enhanced police protection, requiring that many officers have university degrees. Shrewd in the use of media and publicity, she never missed an opportunity to highlight her work in Chacao. A Barbie-type doll appeared in stores, crafted in Sáez's image, with her signature bleached blond hair and wearing a traditional white Venezuelan *liqui-liqui* dress characteristic of the *llanos*. To promote her candidacy, Sáez formed her own party, IRENE (Integration, Renovation and New Hope) and promoted herself as the "peace and children" candidate.

The nation's fractured politics could be seen in the candidates that the parties nominated for the presidency. These included Henrique Salas Römer, a Yale-educated economist and former governor of the state of Carabobo, whose party, *Proyecto Venezuela* (Venezuelan Project), claimed to be independent of existing organizations. Rather than select new leadership, AD's old guard nominated a lackluster longtime stalwart and party head, Luis Alfaro Ucero. Initially dismissed by the mainstream media, Hugo Chávez represented a broad coalition, the *Polo Patriótico* (Patriotic Front), which included an alliance of smaller leftist parties. Earlier in 1997, the MBR-200 had undergone an important transition, leading to the creation of the *Movimiento Quinta Republica* or MVR (Movement of the Fifth Republic). As the candidate of the Polo Patriótico, Chávez blamed the Pact of Punto Fijo for the political state of the country, and insisted on the need to hold a new constitutional convention to replace the existing document drafted in 1961 by the National Congress.

The Polo Patriótico grew to include the PCV, MAS, MEP, and the PPT (a leftist group that had previously split from the Causa R). Many of the party leaders, particularly those in the MAS, opposed Chávez: however, their members rallied behind his candidacy. Besides support from these parties, Chávez increasingly served to channel the existing social movements and the general sense of discontent that existed among diverse classes. The *New York Times* cited a poll taken in September of 1998 that showed that "more than 85 percent of Venezuelans felt cheated out of the benefits of the oil wealth."

With a potential race between Sáez and Chávez, some labeled the contest a choice between "the beauty and the beast."

Without a national apparatus, Sáez accepted the support of COPEI and the endorsement of its previous president Luis Herrera. She also initially received the support of the leftist Causa R which subsequently withdrew its endorsement. As the novelty of her candidacy faded, lacking a comprehensive plan to tackle the country's problems, and having accepted endorsement of COPEI, by May she quickly dropped in the polls. The Alfaro Ucero candidacy also failed to attract much support, receiving less than one percent in a 1997 poll. As the only candidate openly critical of political and economic elites, and promising to reevaluate oil contracts issued under Caldera, Chávez drew attention to his candidacy. Playing on the discontent evident among almost all sectors, by the summer Chávez led in most electoral polls. Some middle- and upper-class sectors began to worry, and one Florida newspaper reported an increase in the purchase of Miami condominiums by wealthy Venezuelans.

Facing a possible Chávez victory, the other political parties actually withdrew their own candidates in order to join together and defeat him. COPEI abandoned Sáez, and AD jettisoned Alfaro Ucero. When Alfaro Ucero refused to step aside, party leaders expelled him from the organization. To prevent a Chávez success, the parties threw their support behind the former governor of Carabobo, Henrique Salas Römer. It was to no avail; on December 6, 1998, receiving fifty-six percent of the vote, Chavez was elected president for the period between 1999 and 2004. Salas Römer came in a distant second with thirty-nine percent; after much fanfare and abandoned by their parties, Sáez marshaled less than three percent and Alfaro Ucero less than one percent. The election of Chávez, a former coup leader, sent shock waves throughout the region and raised concerns in Washington.

Even before his inauguration, Hugo Chávez made important appointments to his cabinet that signaled a shift from previous governments. Breaking with the revolving door that operated between the government, the oil industry, and the private sector, his cabinet choices did not represent Venezuela's dominant economic or political circles. In January of 1999 he designated Alí Rodríguez Araque, a one-time guerrilla who had fought against the Venezuelan government, to head the Ministry of Energy. Rodríguez had criticized PdVSA actions, including Apertura Petrolera begun in 1986, and now assumed a position of oversight of the national oil company. Chávez also named longtime leftist presidential candidate and journalist José Vicente Rangel as minister of foreign affairs. The selection of longtime critics of the status quo clearly signaled that the new Chávez administration sought to reform the political process. Still, some sectors of the political and economic elite discounted Chávez as simply another populist leader that they would eventually be able to control.

Why did Venezuela draft a new constitution in 1999 and what provisions did it include?

As he had promised during the campaign, at his swearing in ceremony on February 2, 1999, Chávez branded the existing constitution "moribund." Constitutional reform would incorporate concrete practical changes as well embodying important political symbolism. On the practical side, it sought to alter power relations, incorporate excluded sectors, and promote the concept of participatory democracy. On a more emblematic level, it denoted a political break with the past and the symbolic refounding of the country. A decision by the Supreme Court cleared the way, and shortly after the inauguration the country embarked on process that would produce a new constitution.

The first step, an election in April 1999 that asked Venezuelans if they wanted to convene a new constitutional convention, was approved by eighty-seven percent, although a significant number of voters abstained. Voters who participated authorized the creation of a Constitutional Assembly that had six months to draft a new document and submit it to voters. The next election, in July 1999, selected individual delegates who would be charged with drafting the new constitution; it included representation by states, with three seats guaranteed for indigenous communities. Although the majority of delegates seeking election represented conservatives, candidates for the MVR and allied parties won a resounding majority, claiming 125 delegates out of the possible 131. The assembly convened in August, suspended the existing congress elected in 1998, and began drafting the new document that was subsequently approved on December 15, 1999 by a margin of seventy-two percent, although once again voter abstention remained high. The government printed pocket size blue copies of the constitution and initiated a campaign to inform people of their new rights.

The constitutional election took place against a backdrop of an unprecedented natural disasters that unfolded in the coastal states of Vargas, Miranda, and the capital of Caracas. Days of torrential tropical rain saturated the hillsides, causing them to give way and unleashing massive landslides that descended on coastal communities, devastating some and entirely obliterating others. Estimates of the human death toll ranged from fifteen to thirty thousand dead. For decades previous governments had allowed people to build rudimentary homes next to streams, on unstable hillsides, or along dry riverbeds. Over time, the mountain streams had amassed debris, creating natural dams, which once breached, sent walls of water down on coastal communities. The area had also been subject to unregulated and largely haphazard growth driven by real estate and construction interests seeking to provide beach homes and apartments for middle- and upper-class residents. The effects of the landslide are still evident: not only did it permanently redefine the Venezuelan coastline, but it forever altered the lives of thousands of people.

The new constitution, which took effect in 2000, changed the name of the country to the Bolivarian Republic of Venezuela, highlighting the importance of Simón Bolívar's ideals and drawing connections to his conception of a Patria Grande (Great Homeland) that included other nations of South America. As importantly, Venezuela proclaimed itself to be a multiethnic and pluricultural state, giving voice to all sectors of society. On the political front, the constitution extended the term of the president from five to six years, allowed for one consecutive reelection, established a vice-president, and, at Chavez's insistence, added a provision whereby the president and other elected officials could be recalled by voters halfway through their terms. It also abolished the bicameral legislative body (congress and senate), creating instead a unicameral national assembly, and allowed military personnel to vote in elections and to assume political positions. Besides the traditional three powers (President, National Assembly, and Judiciary), the constitution also established an electoral power, *Consejo Nacional Electoral*—CNE (National Electoral Commission), to oversee elections. In a move criticized by the opposition, military promotions previously approved by the legislature now became the sole purview of the president. Critics contend that Chávez sought to further concentrate power in the figure of the president and that he sought to guarantee the loyalty of the military.

The constitution gave legal standing for the concept of citizens' power as a check and balance on electoral power, creating special bodies to ensure this process. These reforms broke with the prevailing notions of representative democracy, whereby people entrusted their affairs to politicians they elected every few years. Instead, it sought to empower people, promoting the concept of participatory democracy in which citizens became directly involved in the process of governance. In addition, the state committed itself to the defense of human rights, political pluralism, and access to information. It expanded rights to previously excluded groups, recognizing indigenous people's rights to land, cultural practices, and the use of their own languages. Although it contained strong language on discrimination, the constitution remained surprisingly silent on the rights of Afro-Venezuelans, highlighting the delegates' reluctance to publicly confront this aspect of race in the country. Women's rights expanded significantly, with the constitution providing equal pay for equal work and recognizing housework as productive labor with access to benefits, as well as rights to childcare and the rights of children. In an effort to promote inclusiveness, the constitution established the use of the female and the male voice in all official government documents. It also established access to education, housing, health, and food as inalienable rights guaranteed by the state. The constitution guaranteed the right to work, health and safety concerns, and addressed worker's rights in the management of public enterprises. The environment received special status and the state committed to defend against ecological degradation.

What difficulties did the new constitution face?

Although Venezuela's new constitution represented one of the most progressive constitutions in the world, the principal challenge continued to be the development of efficient mechanisms to educate the populace about the changes and to actually implement many of these new rights. Another difficulty remained the entrenched and traditional political culture that existed in the country. A recalcitrant and stifling government bureaucracy continued to practice old norms, including cronyism, corruption, and special privileges. Another challenge was the generalized lack of experience among many new officials, who for the first time assumed charge of a government ministry or other important public posts. The constant turnover within the staff and leadership at several ministries also became a factor. As the political process radicalized and the government proposed new constitutional changes, groups opposed to Chávez who initially resisted the Constitution of 1999 became its most ardent defenders, insisting on its inviolability.

Even though the country had recently undergone an election, the delegates to the Constitutional Convention approved new mega-elections to be held July 30, 2000, giving voters an opportunity to once again elect all state and municipal officials, the new members of the national assembly, and the president. The mega-election evidenced fractures within the military forces that had participated in the coup of February 1992. Conservative and smaller left-wing and ultra-left-wing parties coalesced behind Francisco Arias Cárdenas, a military commander who had taken part in the coup and had initially been a close Chávez ally. Adopting a moderate tone, Arias Cárdenas, who in 1995 had served as governor of the oil-rich state of Zulia, emphasized his support for private property, decentralized government, and separation of the military from politics. In addition to the presidency, 36,000 candidates vied for 6,100 positions including the national assembly, governorships, and municipal authorities.

On July 30, 2000, Chávez emerged victorious in the election, attaining 59.7 percent of the vote to Arias Cárdenas' 37.5 percent. Delegates of the MVR and other left-wing parties won 104 of the 165 seats in the assembly and sixteen out of twenty-three governorships. The elections confirmed that Chávez's victory in 1998 was not an aberration and underscored the extent to which the political landscape had fundamentally shifted in Venezuela. After the 2002 coup, Arias Cárdenas gradually reconciled with Chávez and eventually became Venezuela's ambassador to the United Nations. He subsequently assumed various other posts in the government and on December 2012 voters once again elected him governor of the state of Zulia.

How did the election of Chávez transform foreign relations?

Having functioned largely in the US political sphere of influence for most of the twentieth century, after the election of

1998 Venezuela sought to chart its own course in international affairs. Since 1999 the Venezuelan government has pursued new foreign policy initiatives, advanced the idea of a multipolar world, assumed a greater role on the international stage, and promoted hemispheric integration. These positions clashed with long-held assumptions about the nature of Venezuela's relations with the world. Critics contended that many sectors in society conflated the oil economy with their own sense of nationalism; the oil economy—with the bulk of Venezuela's production destined for US markets—necessitated good relations with Washington.

Efforts to alter how the nation conducted its foreign affairs heightened tensions between the government and a conservative opposition. Venezuelan relations with the United States did not solely concern the nature of international relations; it also embodied important cultural and social symbolism. For upper- and middle-class sectors of society relations with the United States expressed acceptance of a way of life, defined largely by US values, which served to affirm their own social standing. By not favoring relations with the United States, the Venezuelan government no longer legitimated and promoted these perceptions, but rather became a vocal critic of this lifestyle. The changing nature of the relationship also raised concerns in Washington, long accustomed to having Venezuela follow US initiatives in foreign affairs.

The constitution of 1999 outlined the objectives of Venezuela's new foreign policy. Besides traditional pronouncements about the country's sovereignty in international matters and nonintervention, it explicitly promoted policies that favored the integration of Latin America and the Caribbean, with the goal of "creating a community of nations that would defend the economic, social, cultural, political, and environmental interests of the region." In addition, Venezuela refused to be party to any international agreement that recognized the authority of a supra-national judicial body to resolve disputes, a direct reference to treaties with international lending institutions such as the International Monetary Fund or the World Bank.

Guided by the proposition of a multipolar world, the Venezuelan government sought to establish equitable relations in a post-Cold War era. It affirmed Latin America's role on the world stage and used this approach to prevent the isolation experienced by previous leftist governments such as Guatemala in the 1950s and Cuba in the 1960s. Hoping to strike a balance in its international affairs, Caracas endorsed economic arrangements with China, Cuba, Iran, and Russia, especially in areas such as health, telecommunications, auto manufacturing, oil explorations, and the production of machinery. The Chinese constructed and launched into space Venezuela's two orbiting telecommunication satellites. Iran operates a tractor and car factory in the country and the Russians have become one of the leading arms suppliers of the Venezuelan military. In the United Nations, Venezuela has openly sought the revolving position in the United Nations Security Council. As part of a policy to promote South-South relations, the country expanded diplomatic relations with most countries in Africa and in 2009 hosted the Africa-South America summit.

In the first decade of the 21st century, the Venezuelan government became one of the most fervent critics of Washington's sponsored Free Trade Area of the Americas (FTAA), asserting that it would heighten and institutionalize inequalities already present in economic relations between Latin America and the United States. As evidence, critics of the FTAA pointed to the convulsions evident in Mexico after it signed a similar agreement: the devastation of its rural sector, the outmigration of millions, and the monopolization of the economy by a handful of families. By 2005, Venezuela's position on the FTAA increasingly found support among a majority of South American nations.

How does Washington view developments in Venezuela?

On many fronts, Washington expressed its displeasure with the new Venezuelan government elected in 1998, and the United States' policy towards Venezuela under Bush and under Obama has followed similar tenets. Under the Bush administration, Washington viewed Venezuela's social programs and foreign policy initiatives as a "destabilizing force" and proposed to inoculate Latin America from Caracas in order to stop the spread of the purported contagion. Their strategy rested on the notion that there existed a "good" left consisting of Chile, Brazil, and Uruguay, which was largely pragmatic and open to the United States, and a "bad" left consisting of Venezuela, Bolivia, and Ecuador, largely portrayed as ideological and opposed to the United States. In practice, the levels of cooperation between Latin America countries challenged the US portrayal of the region and highlighted the limitations of an approach that sought to exploit regional differences.

Obama promised a new approach toward Latin America, yet in practice pursued policies that mirrored those adopted during the Bush era. He was welcomed by Latin American leaders in Trinidad at the summit of the Americas in 2009; however, the US refusal to end its embargo against Cuba, as well as their support of the ouster of President Manuel Zelaya of Honduras in June 2009 and unwillingness to characterize it as a coup, soured relations with Venezuela and much of Latin America. In 2007, a cable from the US Ambassador to Chile to the State Department proposed increasing US presence in the region, especially its military power, and holding up Chile as a model for the region.

At the Summit of the Americas held in Cartagena, Colombia, in April 2012, Obama appeared largely isolated, defending the US embargo on Cuba and a drug policy subject to criticism both from allies such as Colombia and Guatemala as well as critics such as Bolivia and Uruguay. Many countries, including Brazil and Ecuador, questioned the viability of future summits if Cuba was not included. Although US policy remains unchanged, the summit revealed that many countries in Latin America are debating alternatives to the current militarization of the drug policy, including legalization of marijuana, a policy already adopted by Uruguay.

What is the importance of regional integration?

A series of social democratic and socialist presidents won elections throughout Latin America in the first decade of the twenty-first century: Luiz Inácio "Lula" da Silva in Brazil in 2002; Nestor Kirchner in Argentina in 2003; Cristina Fernández de Kirchner in 2007 and again 2011; Tabare Vázquez in Uruguay in 2004; Evo Morales in Bolivia and Michelle Bachelet in Chile in 2005; Manuel Zelaya in Honduras and Rafael Correa in Ecuador in 2006; Fernando Lugo in Paraguay in 2008; and Mauricio Funes in El Salvador in 2009. These shifts altered the balance of power in Latin America, boosting hemispheric integration and new foreign policy initiatives. The subsequent reelection of many of these presidents and the election of Dilma Rousseff in Brazil (2010 and 2014), José "Pepe" Mujica in Uruguay (2009), and Salvador Sánchez in El Salvador (2014) confirmed the trend of elected leftist leaders in the region pursuing policy initiatives attuned to their own countries' interests.

While in the past Venezuela had largely ignored the region, the government now asserted the country's role in Latin America. Regional integration became the central tenet of the Venezuelan foreign policy toward Latin America. Integration refers to efforts by countries to forge economic ties and make policy decisions that prioritize the interests of Latin America. It found expression in the formation of new regional associations that did not include Washington, such as the Union of South American Nations (UNASUR), the Community of Latin American and Caribbean Countries (CELAC), and Bolivarian Alliance for the Peoples of the Americas (ALBA). The rise of these new hemispheric groups produced an unparalleled level of cooperation among Latin American states while diminishing the traditional role of the Organization of American States (OAS), where the United States exercised significant influence. Different perspectives persist and countries still pursue their own interests, but the level of consultation and cooperation among governments, and as importantly, among social movements in South America is unprecedented.

The process of regional integration proceeded along two parallel paths and included broad regional organizations representing all governments irrespective of their political philosophy and other bodies that primarily represent left or socialist governments. The most dramatic example of regional integration is reflected in the founding of UNASUR in 2008, which despite personal or ideological differences included all the countries of South America. The founding of UNASUR, of which Venezuela was an early proponent, was the result of meetings between heads of state, starting in the early 2000s, that explored the formation of a South American Community of Nations. The first energy summit of South American presidents in April of 2007, convened on the Venezuelan island of Margarita, served to advance the formation of UNASUR.

With a rotating permanent secretariat, UNASUR includes meetings of heads of states, foreign ministers, and several councils that oversee defense, culture, science, environment, and other matters. UNASUR also founded the Bank of the South to provide credit to member states without the onerous conditions imposed by international lending agencies and established a regional security apparatus to promote its own independent approach toward drug trafficking.

On December 2 and 3, 2011, Latin American and Caribbean nations convened in Caracas to formally establish the Community of Latin American and Caribbean States (CELAC), which includes all countries of the hemisphere except the United States and Canada. The foundation for the conference had been established at a meeting in 2010 in Cancun, Mexico, although the early roots of this organization can be traced to efforts in the 1980s by Venezuela, Panama, Mexico, and Colombia to find a peaceful solution to the civil wars in Central America amid growing US military intervention in the region. Eventually the original members of the Contadora group (named for the island on which they met) expanded to include Argentina, Brazil, Peru, and Uruguay. In 1986, these countries met in Rio de Janeiro and formed the RIO Group, laying the groundwork for an all-Latin-American-and-Caribbean group.

At the broadest levels, political changes after 2000 invigorated the RIO group and established it as the principal forum for Latin American nations regardless of their political orientation. An example of the extent to which these new bodies had begun to act independently of the United States occurred in the aftermath of Colombia's incursion into Ecuadorian territory in March 2008. Claiming to be in pursuit of rebels, Colombian military forces entered Ecuadorian territory and killed several guerrillas. Venezuela and Ecuador sent troops to their border with Colombia and tensions mounted. Within days, the XX RIO summit meeting occurred in the Dominican Republic and quickly eased tensions, without US involvement, and managed to establish a dialogue between the various countries. The actions of the XX RIO summit sidelined the OAS and the United States, traditionally expected to play a major role in disputes in the hemisphere, thus highlighting the extent to which Latin American countries now operated independently of Washington.

Efforts by the Venezuelan government to promote alternative forms of integration included the formation of ALBA. Propelled by an explicit leftist agenda, ALBA's first summit was held in Havana in 2004, and by 2009 it grew to include Bolivia, Ecuador, Honduras (before the coup in 2009), Nicaragua, San Vincent, Antigua, Barbuda, and Dominica. ALBA incorporates Simón Bolívar's vision of Latin America as the Patria Grande (Great Homeland), forming a series of alliances that address economic, cultural, medical, and educational initiatives. One of the central features of ALBA is the creation of the Bank of Alba, similar to the Bank of the South, which offers member nations alternative forms of credit while proposing the use of an alternative electronic currency known as the Sucre. ALBA has become an important left-wing bloc within the process of regional integration, in some cases representing a unified position within the UNASUR, the CELAC, the OAS, and other international summits. Under the present scenario, the United States is no longer the central foreign policy concern for Venezuela or many of the nations of the region. Operating in concert or independently, these countries have charted a new foreign policy that now more closely reflects their own national interests.

Efforts at regional integration also include the rise of alternative media outlets that focus on developments transpiring in Latin America, Africa, and Asia, and no longer exclusively cover only the United States or Europe. At the center of these efforts is *Telesur* (Television of the South), a new regional media initiative involving many of the countries of UNASUR, that transmits from Caracas. With the motto "*Nuestro norte es el sur*" ("The south is our focus"), Telesur provides an alternative to foreign media outlets, which only occasional cover events in Latin America or at times tend to echo concerns expressed by Washington. The coverage Telesur provided during the 2009 coup in Honduras, at a time when other outlets largely ignored the event, drew international attention to the network. As importantly, Telesur provides coverage of and an outlet to social movements that are typically absent from mainstream media. The alternative media project also includes la Radio del Sur, (Radio of the South), which links with existing stations in Latin America.

How did oil policy in Venezuela change after Chávez's election?

During the first years of Chávez's presidency, oil prices hovered at less than $8 a barrel, the lowest price in decades. To buttress world prices, Venezuela sought to reclaim its historic role within OPEC and its oversight over PdVSA, the national oil conglomerate. Venezuela assumed the leadership position of OPEC between 2001 and 2002 and hosted its summit meeting in Caracas. In August 2000, Chávez visited all ten fellow OPEC nations; critics at home and in the United States accused him of cavorting with terrorists. The critics lost sight of the fact that the visit to the OPEC countries, the first to the region by a Venezuelan head of state, sought to increase the price of oil, the country's principal export product. During the trip, Chávez personally extended invitations to the leaders of the OPEC nations to attend the summit and lobbied to raise oil prices. At the 2002 summit in Caracas, OPEC affirmed support for quotas assigned to member nations that in the past Venezuela had regularly ignored and adopted an acceptable range within which oil prices could fluctuate. The Venezuelan government also pushed OPEC to adopt more explicit social policies: the final declaration addressed the issue of the insurmountable debt that strangled many Third World countries and expressed concerns regarding conditions of poverty that many nations faced. Through its actions, the Chávez government helped revitalize OPEC and affirmed Venezuela's role on the international stage.

Besides OPEC, the government turned its attention to Venezuela's oil industry, previously nationalized in 1976 under Carlos Andres Pérez. As discussed previously, the 1976 nationalization law remained fraught with loopholes allowing foreign companies to continue to operate in the country through service contracts or in advisory roles. Moreover, the nationalization in 1976 had done little to alter the existing corporate culture within PdVSA that projected the firm as an international oil conglomerate operating in Venezuela. In addition, during the 1990s the previously mentioned Apertura Petrolera (Oil Opening) had increased the foreign presence in the oil industry and expanded its role in the Orinoco basin. Under Chávez, the government sought to complete the

nationalization of the oil industry, close the loopholes established by the 1976 law, reassert state control over the petroleum industry, and bring the oil conglomerate PdVSA under
the control of the government.

Much of the tension revolved around PdVSA's upper management team; steeped in the tradition of the foreign companies,
they viewed the government as an obstacle to the independence and operation of the enterprise. As they had historically,
PdVSA managers portrayed themselves as experts, and the
government and the larger public as either ignorant or inept
on oil matters. This is a legacy that drew from the decades-
long experience with US oil companies, in which foreigners
possessed the knowledge to operate the oil companies and the
Venezuelans became passive recipients of this information.
From this perspective, the managers created a false dichotomy
in which they sought to protect a profitable private enterprise
from a corrupt government and an undiscerning general public. As part of this argument, PdVSA managers, and even some
employees, asserted that they had attained their positions as a
result of personal merit. In theory, the defense of a meritocracy
sought to accentuate divisions between the oil sector that purportedly represented personal initiative and sacrifice and others that relied on government patronage. Employees of PdVSA
protested by appropriating public spaces, naming the square
outside the old Shell/Maraven building in Chuao the "Plaza of
Meritocracy," while others formed a civic organization known
as *Gente de Petróleo* or People of Oil. Although the idea of meritocracy served to rally middle-class sectors and others in the
opposition, the actual experience of the oil industry contra-
dicted this notion. The industry had historically favored hiring from within, since it ensured that employees had already
undergone a degree of acculturation and had some exposure
to corporate culture.

The central concern of the government related to the dwin-
dling profits PdVSA provided the Venezuelan state. During
the Caldera presidency, PdVSA had increasingly reduced the

percentage of profits it allocated to the government, claiming the need to pursue international initiatives and reinvest into the company a sizable amount of the capital they generated. For the government, correcting this imbalance was central since it needed these resources to fund social programs. In order to determine the nature of agreements entered into during the Apertura Petrolera, the Chávez government had to establish control over PdVSA. Subsequently, it proceeded to renegotiate the agreements signed with foreign oil companies during the early 1990s. Under the Apertura, Venezuela did not include production from the Orinoco basin as part of its OPEC-mandated output. Moreover, foreign firms paid royalties based on the 1943 law with rates as low as 16 2/3 percent.

On November 13, 2001, making use of special powers granted by the congress, the Chávez government approved a new hydrocarbon law that placed oil unequivocally under state control. The government continued reviewing existing contracts, and by 2007 had taken a majority stake in the principal heavy crude projects in the Orinoco basin. As a result some US companies such as Exxon Mobil and Conoco Phillips eventually left Venezuela and filed lawsuits claiming that the government's actions amounted to a new nationalization without compensation. Chinese, Indian, Russian, and other US energy companies (including Chevron Texaco) continue to operate in the Orinoco basin. With the inclusion of the Orinoco basin— covering the states of Guárico, Anzoátegui, Monagas, and Delta Amacuro—OPEC certified that Venezuelan reserves reached 296 billion barrels of oil, surpassing Saudi Arabia and becoming the world's largest. With the inclusion of the larger Orinoco fields, oil reserves could potentially reach 513 billion barrels. PdVSA has also worked to diversify its markets, no longer depending exclusively on the United States, to whom it had been selling approximately 900,000 barrels a day. When Chávez assumed the presidency, Venezuela did not sell oil to China; in 2012 it sold over 600,000 barrels a day to the Asian country. By April 2014 China and India were receiving

959,000 barrels a day and Asia became the leading market for Venezuelan oil.

Taken as a whole, oil and gas supplies in South America represent one of the largest reservoirs of energy in the world. Venezuela also adopted a new oil policy toward Latin America in 2005, creating Petro Caribe, which provides oil to Caribbean and Central America member nations under long-term credit arrangements. Cuba in particular receives approximately 100,000 barrels of oil a day. Venezuela also established Petro Sur to promote cooperation on energy matters between state oil companies in Brazil, Uruguay, Argentina, and Venezuela. Working through community organizations in the United States, Venezuela has also provided heating oil to low-income communities in the US northeast.

Why did conservatives resort to a coup against the government in April 2002?

With consecutive defeats at the polls in 1998 and again in the mega-elections in 2000, the Venezuelan opposition parties entered a period of disarray. New parties emerged, including *Un Nuevo Tiempo* (A New Time) in 1999 and *Primero Justicia* (Justice First) in 2000 that brought together some former members of AD, COPEI, and others. These parties proposed an eclectic set of values that ranged from traditional neoliberal economic approaches to vague notions of humanism and justice. However, they lacked a national structure, tended initially to represent white upper- and middle-class sectors, and did not have a broad following. Lacking a real grassroots network, many of these organizations and their self-proclaimed leaders relied on a largely sympathetic media to disseminate their message and promote their presence.

Increasingly, the commercial media, both print and broadcast, dropped all pretenses of objectivity and began in large measure to fill the void left by the parties and to assume the mantle of the opposition. Shows on television outlets such

Radio Caracas Televisión, Venevisión, and the cable channel Globovisión increasingly gave voice and provided cohesion to the disenchanted opposition. Since 2002 the opposition Globovisión television channel had countered Chávez's broadcasts with its own *Alo Ciudadano* (Hello Citizen) program, which transmitted every day and openly criticized government policies. Newspapers with national circulation, such as *El Nacional* and *El Universal*, openly slanted their reporting to support the opposition.

Beyond political programming, increasing opposition to the Chávez government may also have been driven by economic concerns, since media outlets sought to ensure a middle- and upper-class audience that would attract advertisers. Nonetheless, most in the opposition received their information and framed their ideas almost exclusively from conservative media sources, increasingly giving rise to an echo chamber that constantly reinforced their views. Supporters of the government also reflected this tendency, obtaining news from newly developed television, print, and digital sources sympathetic to the government. The selective reception of information reinforced already held views and increased polarization.

The opposition blamed the government for addressing class and racial issues, suggesting that these acrimonious matters had been artificially manufactured by Chávez to rally mass support among the poor. To view race and class as artificially manufactured, however, reflected a lack of knowledge of Venezuelan history and demonstrated the insular lifestyle that certain sectors enjoyed. Increasingly, this politically conservative perspective yearned for the pre-Chavez era and fueled a perception that Venezuela was on the brink of collapse, a country spiraling out of control. In their reporting on Venezuela, the US-based media tended to bolster this view, portraying a country in which civil conflict appeared eminent.

Another important voice for the opposition came from *Fedecámaras*, the national association of chambers of commerce that insisted that government policies adversely affected its members. The leadership of the *Confederación de Trabajadores de Venezuela* (CTV)—the national labor confederation historically associated with AD—also added its voice to the opposition forces organizing against Chávez. This was not the first time that the CTV and Fedecamaras cooperated; in 1997 they worked together to draft a Labor Law Reform. In particular, the leadership of the oil workers union, traditionally a privileged sector of the labor force enjoying the highest wages and benefits in the country, became openly critical of the government's efforts to reign in PdVSA. Ironically, business interests, union leaders, and television personalities became the public face of the opposition. The tenor of the discourse between both sides deteriorated: opposition leaders often used racial epitaphs to describe the president, and Chávez increasingly referred to them as a squalid elite that consciously placed their interests above those of the nation.

The adoption of a package of forty-nine laws in November 2001 that included the oil legislation and agrarian reform, during a period when the national assembly had granted Chávez special presidential powers common to previous administrations, became the rallying cry of the opposition. Claiming the need to place more land under agricultural production and make it available to rural producers, the agrarian law targeted unused land. Many landowners kept extensive tracts of land fallow, viewing it as a long-term investment. For the rural population, however, this practice limited their access to land and kept them dependent on landowners for employment. Chávez's opposition claimed the agrarian law ignored the preeminence of private property established in the constitution of 1999. Earlier they had also reacted to an educational decree intended to create a group of inspectors to report on the state of education. The opposition insisted that the decree represented a threat to religious education and therefore promoted political indoctrination, although none of these matters appeared in the pronouncement. The passage of these laws served to reinvigorate the opposition and their assertion that Chávez lacked strong popular support to pursue these goals. With the open encouragement of the private media and the business sectors that closed down enterprises and their stores in solidarity, the opposition increasingly staged large public protests. In early December 2001, during a planned national strike, opposition leaders publicly called for Chávez to resign. *Cacerolazos*, the clanging of pots and pans from middle- and upper-middle-class neighborhoods (a tactic used first against Salvador Allende in Chile), became common every time the president did a *cadena* (literally a chain)—a public address to the nation that television stations are required to transmit. Enterprising *buhoneros* (street vendors) actually produced a CD recording of clanging pots and pans for individuals who still wanted to publicly register their discontent by playing it close to a window. Chávez claimed to use *cadenas* in order to broadcast his message, since private media regularly presented a one-sided view of the government's actions.

By 2002, cracks in the president's coalition had emerged; some former allies openly criticized the government, further encouraging the opposition. In addition, a small number of active duty military officers became emboldened and publicly spoke at protests against the president, accusing him of treason. The media gave these pronouncements ample coverage and rumors of a possible coup circulated widely.

On April 9, 2002, the opposition called for a general strike and a series of protest marches. Some television stations exhorted viewers to participate and provided live coverage of the activities. On April 11 an opposition demonstration that began and was intended to end in eastern Caracas deviated from its course upon exhortations from opposition leaders and proceeded instead toward the presidential palace at Miraflores where pro-government forces congregated in the western part of the city. As the march approached Miraflores, snipers shot into the crowd, killing nineteen people and wounding hundreds. As Chávez addressed the nation on television and called for calm, the private channels split the screen to show the shootings as the president spoke, fueling the impression that the government condoned the violence. Despite the fact that the dead included both Chávez supporters and members of the opposition, the media portrayed it as a premeditated action on the part of government. A group of military officers who had been preparing for a coup used the pretext of the bloodshed to announce their decision to rise in arms against the president and issued an ultimatum that he resign or they would attack the presidential palace.

Intense negotiations followed. Chávez insisted on the safety of his personnel and the right to address the nation, which, remembering what happened in 1992, the generals leading the coup denied. Some of Chávez's allies advocated fighting their way out of the palace. Without formally resigning, early in the morning of April 12, 2002, Chávez agreed to be taken prisoner. The military faction involved in the coup eventually transferred him to Fuerte Tiuna, the principal military base in Caracas, and subsequently to the island of Orchilla, an isolated base on the coast of Venezuela. In the early morning, Lucas Rincón, the inspector general of the armed forces, announced to the country that Chávez had resigned the presidency.

Having ceased transmission as the events at the presidential palace unfolded, the commercial television channels returned to the air on the morning of April 12 and announced that Venezuela had a new president. Bypassing the constitutional vice-president, Diosdado Cabello, the military announced that Pedro Carmona, the head of Fedecamaras, had assumed the presidency. In a largely celebratory event, and surrounded by Catholic Church officials and leading business and political figures, Carmona formally assumed the presidency on the afternoon of April 12. Over four hundred leading Venezuelan opposition figures signed the now-infamous Carmona decree, formally aligning themselves with the coup's objectives. Almost immediately the coup government appointed a new cabinet and began to dismantle the Chávez-era policies, dissolving all elected bodies—including the assembly, governorships, and municipal authorities—and revoking the forty-nine laws passed earlier.

As these events unfolded, the military˙sought to arrest Chávez's close supporters who had escaped from the presidential palace and members of his cabinet. The coup leaders also sought to control the media throughout the nation, forcibly shutting down the government channel *Venezolana de Televisión* (VTV) as well as community radio stations.

Ultimately, the coup proved short lived. The opposition had underestimated the popular support the president and his administration enjoyed, including support in the military, and the extent to which the political conditions in the country had changed. Almost immediately following the coup, the Venezuelan social movements that had backed the president began to coordinate resistance throughout Venezuela. Additionally, other forces that might have supported the coup resented the fact that the new government abolished all elected offices. In other cases, average Venezuelans distrusted official pronouncements and questioned the official versions of the events. The strange programming on the television channels, in some cases reruns of dubbed US cartoons, added to the climate of uncertainty. On April 12, having gained access to a cellular phone, Chávez called his daughter María Gabriela and informed her of his whereabouts. The account of the coup began to unravel as several radio stations, including the Catholic *Fe y Alegria* (Faith and Happiness), offered a counternarrative to what the commercial media reported, indicating that Chávez had not resigned.

Within the military, officers in charge of paratroopers, armored units, and even pilots of the F-16s supplied by the United States openly opposed the illegal break in the constitutional order and supported the president. More importantly, they refused to concede their posts to supporters of the coup, and began to communicate with each other and with those organizing the popular resistance. It quickly became evident

that some upper-echelon elements of the military had orchestrated the coup against the government and that the military
itself remained sharply divided. Crowds began to concentrate at various points in Caracas and in the interior, and at
night the customary clanging of pots and pans emanating
from poorer neighborhoods announced support for Chávez,
not the opposition. Attacks on businesses and the raiding of
stores also transpired with some frequency. Sensing trouble,
Carmona convened all the directors of the private television
channels, seeking their support to avoid transmitting the perception of a crisis.

On the international front, the coup plotters expected
the United States' recognition. They were elated to hear Ari
Fleischer, the White House press secretary, proclaim that
Chávez had brought the coup on himself. In addition, an edi-
torial in the *New York Times* on April 13 asserted, "With yes-
terday's resignation of President Hugo Chávez, Venezuelan
democracy is no longer threatened by a would-be dictator."
Holding a summit in Costa Rica, the nations of the RIO group
did not follow Washington's lead and condemned the coup,
requesting an emergency meeting of the OAS to address
the issue. Shortly thereafter, the OAS also condemned the
alteration of constitutional order. Except for support from El
Salvador's right-wing government, the Carmona coup government found itself completely isolated in the region.

By Saturday April 13 tens of thousands of people surrounded the presidential palace and the base at Fuerte Tiuna
demanding the return of their president. Inside Miraflores the
young soldiers that formed the honor guard welcomed the
protestors, waving the Venezuelan flag. Officers in charge of
the honor guard had established contact with several commanders who had remained loyal to the constitution. Inside,
the honor guard overwhelmed the squad protecting Carmona,
and the would-be president escaped out a side door.

Facing mounting popular opposition and a rebellion within
the military, the coup collapsed and Chávez returned to power.

The opposition had once again miscalculated the extent to which the political landscape had fundamentally changed in Venezuela. The right-wing government, willing to dispense with the democratic structures of the nation's government, lasted less than forty-eight hours.

Why did the opposition attempt to shut down oil production?

The coup's defeat did not deter the conservative opposition's efforts to topple Chávez and turn back the political process underway in Venezuela. Leaders of PdVSA and the CTV (labor federation), many of whom participated in the coup, declared a *paro civico nacional* (a national work stoppage) on December 2, 2002. It soon became obvious that the strike leaders aimed to shut down oil production, deny the government income, and once again try to force Chávez's resignation. Evidence of sabotage of oil installations also subsequently surfaced. Beyond the immediate damage, shutdown of oil wells generates long-term consequences, since inactivity can significantly set back future extraction of oil. As part of the conspiracy, a number of tanker captains anchored their ships at strategic locations in Lake Maracaibo to block the waterway. Without trained personnel to manage operations, over forty foreign tankers remained off the coast, refusing to dock at PdVSA installations to load oil. With oil beginning to reach thirty dollars a barrel, losses mounted for the Venezuelan oil company and by extension the government.

On matters of oil, two issues framed much of the dispute between the government and the opposition forces, one economic and the other, equally potent, largely symbolic. The government's authority over PdVSA assured its control over the principal source of revenue in the country and over the powerful symbol of Venezuelan modernity and prosperity for a segment of the middle and upper sectors of society. PdVSA thus not only was a guarantor of state revenues; it was also a guarantor of a distinct way of life. Having lost control of the government, conservatives saw PdVSA as a powerful tool with which to challenge the government, exert pressure, and restrict access to needed resources.

Beyond PdVSA, the business sector joined in by shutting their operations and forcing employees out of work. From the beginning, what the opposition called a national strike took on the appearance of a lockout, as workers were refused access to their places of employment. For hundreds of small-and medium-sized businesses pressured to shut down the timing of the lockout proved critical, since it had a direct impact on their ability to take advantage of increased purchases during the December holidays. Without access to fuel, the country came to virtual standstill. At a time when thousands of Venezuelans travel to visit family, airlines, bus companies, and taxis cut back or canceled service. Long lines of drivers at gas stations seeking to purchase the remaining supplies of gasoline generated the sense of chaos the conservative opposition forces had anticipated. For the opposition, creating the perception—if not conditions—of ungovernability and popular discontent proved central to their strategy to oust a government they had been unable to defeat at the ballot box.

Backed by an order from the Supreme Court to reinitiate activities, the government ordered employees to return to work or risk losing their jobs and, in some cases, their homes, since many continued to live in oil camps owned by the company. For many of these individuals, beyond a direct source of employment, work in the oil industry constituted a way of life and a benefits package not shared by the large majority of Venezuelans. The opposition had gambled that the government would capitulate, believing it could not regain control of the oil company without the striking managers and workers. Without a doubt, those on strike represented years of experience and collective knowledge about the internal workings of the Venezuelan oil industry. However, the opposition had once again underestimated the level of support for the government among oil workers and the population, as well as the ability of the social movements to organize in defense of PdVSA. Moreover, it didn't calculate that many employees would either refuse to abandon their jobs or would willingly return to work and help reestablish operations. International support also played a role in buttressing the position of the government. Brazil, which had recently elected Lula to the presidency (although he had not yet assumed office), sold 520,000 barrels of oil to Venezuela, reducing shortages in late December. Opposition leaders predictably decried the sale as "Brazilian interference" in Venezuela's internal affairs.

The most symbolic event that marked the turning point of the strike occurred when the government dispatched a new captain and crew and regained control of the tanker *Pilin León* (named after a former Miss Venezuela/Miss World winner, subsequently renamed Negra Matea) that blocked the principal traffic lanes in Lake Maracaibo, an event broadcast live on television. Similar operations took place in La Guaira, Caracas's principal port, where tankers had also anchored at sea. Government supporters also stood guard at PdVSA installations to protect them from further disruptions. As the pace of production accelerated, fuel trucks protected by the National Guard resumed deliveries to service stations.

By late December it became obvious that the so-called strike had failed to dislodge the president from office. The conservative opposition's actions were, however, successful in having a dramatic impact on the economy and the population as a whole. Some estimates indicate the country lost upwards of fourteen billion dollars in oil revenue, plunging it into a recession. In addition the economy contracted significantly and unemployment increased, as did inflation. Shortages of food proved common and private business sectors, unable to operate during the holidays, lost significant revenue.

Despite the evident worsening economic conditions, the national strike formally continued until February 2003, when it fizzled out and normal economic activity fully resumed. In reality, by late December some businesses had begun to open, leaving the opposition without much alternative. Hoping to save face, they timed the end of the stoppage to a new effort that sought to make use of the provision in the 1999 Constitution to recall elected officials. They devised a campaign they called the *firmazo* (the great signature gathering), collecting signatures from the electorate to trigger the recall of the president. According to the process outlined in the constitution they needed to collect the signatures of twenty percent of the electorate, amounting to 2.4 million voters. National television channels and radio not only promoted the *firmazo*, urging viewers and listeners to take part, but also provided daylong coverage of the activities. In the end, the tactic failed to achieve its goal; the CNE ruled that the collection of signatures had not occurred before the midpoint of the president's administration as mandated by the constitution. Moreover, under official scrutiny many of the signatures appeared forged and others represented deceased voters.

International mediation by the Carter Center, the OAS, a group of friendly Latin American nations and the UN facilitated formal dialogue between the opposition and the government that enabled the recall process included in the Venezuelan constitution. The government proclaimed this a victory since it implied the opposition's de facto acceptance of the constitution of 1999, and assumed an electoral avenue to resolve differences rather than coups or work stoppages. The opposition announced a *re-afirmazo* (a second signature gathering) starting on November 28 and lasting until December 1. This time, however, citizens would have to show their *cédula*, a national identification card used since the 1940s, and leave an imprint of their fingerprints to verify their signature. The CNE slowly processed the request, allowing additional days for *reparos* (literally, repairs) in May of 2004 in which those whose names appeared truncated or unclear could re-sign. Finally in June of 2004 the CNE, after many delays, confirmed the authenticity of the signatures and authorized a recall election to be held on August 15, 2004.

In preparation for the recall election, the government created an electoral coalition named *Maisanta*, after a late-nineteenth-century rebel leader (Chávez's great-grandfather), which brought together social movements, leftist parties, and supporters of the government. The opposition continued to coalesce under an umbrella organization, the *Coordinadora Democrática* (Democratic Coordinating body), which had also organized the previous work stoppage. Though they remained united in their desire to oust Chávez, the lack of internal consensus limited their ability to designate a candidate to challenge the president. Despite some of the private polls claiming an uphill battle for the president, throughout the recall campaign Chávez gradually improved his standing among numerous sectors of the population. After a hard-fought campaign, in an election with over a seventy percent level of participation and audited by international observers, Chávez supporters overwhelmingly defeated the recall, with the president receiving fifty-nine percent of the vote to the opposition's forty-one percent, a margin of eighteen percent.

The attempted recall of a president represented an unprecedented action on the world stage. Moreover, during the recall the CNE introduced touchscreen ballot machines into the electoral process that both generated an electronic vote and produced a paper ballot that the voter could check against the result in their voting booth. In addition to an official audit, citizen and international observers participated in the audit of the vote. Government officials, opposition members, and international observers tested the machines before the elections to assure the absence of improprieties and the National Electoral Commission controlled all the access codes. As they had in the past, many in the opposition overestimated their own position and could not face the results, refusing to accept them and raising claims of fraud.

In the aftermath of the recall, tensions increased when Luis Tascón, a member of the assembly, published on his website the names of those who had signed the petition against

Chávez. Tascón claimed to have bought the list from Sumate, a leading opposition organization. Charges quickly followed that the government used the list to dismiss public employees and deny company contracts. Although Chávez eventually condemned the list in 2005, the existence of the list added to the climate of polarization in the country. (Tascón was expelled from the pro-Chávez movement in 2007 for other reasons.)

After the defeat of the recall election, recrimination among opposition circles led to the fracture of the Coordinadora Democrática. In private communiqués the United States embassy in Caracas worried how the anti-Chávez forces would forge unity after the collapse of the umbrella group. The embassy concluded that rather than continue to build unity the "*coordinadora* members are choosing to shoot their wounded." The disarray that the United States embassy feared became evident in 2005 when AD decided not to participate in midterm elections, alleging lack of trust in the process. Soon other parties followed AD's lead and abstained from the elections, hoping that by boycotting the process they might strip the government of legitimacy. The opposition recognized that midterm elections traditionally drew a small percentage of voters to the polls, and they made use of the low levels of participation to claim that their followers had heeded their call not to vote. In retrospect, some party leaders now consider the abstention a mistake, for the election predictably gave the government supporters absolute control in the national assembly with which they could now more quickly approve new laws and social reforms.

What was the basis of Chávez's support?

It is not a simple task to characterize people who supported the Chávez government. Adherents include those drawn from diverse social backgrounds, historical experiences, and political orientations. What is apparent, however, is that they are not simply anonymous uneducated masses drawn by the rhetorical persuasion of a charismatic leader. They are also not merely supporting the government because they are recipients of state-funded social programs. Although some client-patron relations still persist, as they do in any society, these alone cannot explain the degree and intensity of support that the government has enjoyed. Popular mobilizations to reinstate Chávez after the 2002 coup, and the support for the government despite the hardships of a national work stoppage and efforts at destabilization, speak to a level of support and investment people have made in the current political project. A new level of political participation, knowledge of the country's history, civic engagement, and national pride is now evident in Venezuela. The national flag, previously relegated to Independence Day, is now displayed regularly, becoming a contested symbol appropriated by both supporters of the government and the opposition.

The appearance of Chávez on the national stage during the 1990s served to consolidate diverse left-wing trends that had been active in community-based movements and among workers, women's organizations, and groups of intellectuals. It also gave voice to the struggles of people of color, the indigenous, and those of African heritage long marginalized by a discourse on a supposedly thorough miscegenation (*café con leche*) and the existence of a purported racial democracy. The other sector, from which Chávez personally ascended, represents the legacy of a nationalist and leftist trend within the military evident in the leadership of the insurgent movements of the 1960s. In addition, untold numbers of people who had lost faith in the political process became reenergized and acquired new hope in response to the alternative political project that Chávez proposed. These sectors, disparate but similarly disenfranchised, took ownership of the social programs initiated by the government and demonstrated a new sense of personal empowerment and political involvement in defense of their new rights.

Women in particular have played a central role in the current political process. The constitution of 1999 recognized women's rights to equal pay, declared housework as productive labor, acknowledged the importance of childcare, and included the female subject in public speech and documents. Beyond constitutional reform, there is now a cabinet-level Department for Women and Gender Equality (previously Family) that oversees the *InaMujer* (Institute for Women). The Institute for Women is responsible for promoting policies that seek to incorporate women into all aspects of society and defends their political and personal rights. In addition, the Bank for Women's Development provides micro-credits to fund economic projects managed by women.

The traditional nuclear family has continued to change, and female-headed households have grown to represent nearly forty percent of all families in Venezuela. In these homes, women are the breadwinners and caretakers of their families. Therefore it is not surprising to see women involved in all facets of the contemporary political arena, especially the avenues open for community organizing or new government programs. Women play a predominant role in neighborhood associations, the communes, and the social missions, where they hold most leadership positions. Since 2000, the number of women in the armed forces, both as soldiers and officers, has increased significantly. Women are also represented in mayoral office, the state and national assembly, the federal government, and have comprised one third of the presidential cabinet. At one time in 2006, the heads of the National Assembly, the Electoral Commission, the Attorney General, and the Supreme Court were all women. This predominance became fodder for a conservative newspaper that printed sexualized images of women in power as cabaret dancers, describing them as "the powerful women of the pretty revolution." Despite these attacks, the presence of women in the public arena and in positions of power continues to gain broader acceptance. What remains unclear however is the extent to which the empowerment of women has transformed social and familial relations. Not surprisingly, as an expanding political force, a significant number of women have shown support for the government.

Venezuela has historically had a strong legacy of leftwing and grassroots social movements. After the experience of the 1960s, and the failure of the armed insurgency against the government, many individuals and groups reconsidered their strategy and turned their attention to organizing among sectors of society that lived on the margins of Venezuela's oil wealth. The striking differences that existed between those that benefited from the nation's oil resources and those that survived in makeshift *ranchos* (shacks) on the edges of the petroleum economy provided fertile ground for social activists.

As discussed, the urban poor typically lived on hillsides that shape the fractured valleys surrounding Caracas, the ravines of the Mérida plateau, or the expansive outskirts of cities such as Maracaibo. Barrios such as Jesús Felix Ribas in Caracas, Pueblo Nuevo in Mérida, or Concepción (Cañada de Urdaneta) outside of Maracaibo are typical of this experience. Normally people seeking to improve their lives migrated from the interior and settled in unused or unclaimed land. Other family members and extended family soon followed. Their homes, precariously built structures constructed with a collection of sheets of zinc, block, plastic, and even cardboard, seldom enjoyed services like electricity and water. With limited access to resources, at times neighbors resorted to forming community kitchens to address basic nutritional needs. To acquire essential necessities neighbors had to improvise and petition the government for services. The ubiquitous light pole, with dozens of unregulated lines strewn in multiple directions to provide electricity to nearby homes, typifies this improvisation. Gradually homes acquired a degree of permanence as block and mortar replaced zinc and cardboard.

This process of engaging the government provided fertile ground for collective action and served as training ground for innumerable neighborhood councils and organizations that flourished in urban areas. In established neighborhoods such as the sprawling 23 de Enero and the Sarría neighborhood, residents organized to obtain services such as building maintenance, trash removal, and a means of dealing with crime. As these community organizations matured, gained experiences, and asserted political demands, they became protagonists in the defense of their neighborhoods.

Another area of support for the Chávez government emerged from an unlikely source: the military. Venezuela's military differs from similar institutions in Latin America that had been the sole domain of the landed or political elites—throughout much of its twentieth-century history, its officers and noncommissioned personnel have been drawn from diverse socioeconomic sectors of the population. The military provided many of these young officers a way to climb the social ladder. In the military they found like-minded colleagues who expressed concern about the direction of the country and the corruption evident in the political class. Efforts by officers to forge a military-civic alliance that included progressive social forces also drew from historical experiences addressed previously. Since 1999 the government has sought to integrate the military into society, giving it a role to play in social programs and anti-poverty campaigns.

The other source of support for Chávez resides in the political and social mobilizations that have occurred in the past fourteen years. Thousands of people participate in *consejos comunales* (community councils) where they grapple with needs in their communities and then participate in resolving the issues they have identified, promoting the ideal of community self-governance. The government allocates funds to address the needs that the councils have identified. Participation in the mission programs has also been transformative for many of who have organized to receive services. Participants in literacy, health, construction, education, or other programs derive a sense of empowerment from claiming new rights. The success or failure of the programs depends in large part on the

participation of those who benefit from the venture. The government also enjoys support within some segments of the
middle classes who are motivated by a moral commitment to
improve people's conditions, and a basic nationalist pride that
seeks to advance the nation as a whole. This support within
the middle class is an important factor beyond just the number
of people involved, for these sympathizers include intellectuals, professionals, trained artists, and others whose talents
have greatly aided the overall movement. Thus besides those
who participate directly in and benefit directly from social
programs, there is a palpable sense of empowerment from
diverse sections of society and recognition of rights that previously did not exist.

Chávez developed a unique bond with many of his supporters. Since 1992, when he took responsibility for the failure of the coup, he emerged as a different type of leader. His
defense of the poor and critique of the wealthy and the persistent issue of state corruption increased the perception of
Chávez as unafraid to challenge the existing power structure.
Regularly mocked by the opposition and the national and
international press, his television show *Alo Presidente* (Hello
President), an often rambling program that Chávez hosted on
Sundays, allowed him to connect with supporters in ways that
leaders had not done in the past. Transmitted from different
locations, the program typically sought to highlight the work
of farming or cattle cooperatives, communal production units,
and neighborhood associations. With Chávez as moderator,
the program was a mixture of personal accounts, reports from
ministers, and even included cabinet changes and the launching of new policies or programs. Mr. Chavez's ability to hold
forth for so long revealed the bombastic and pedantic side of
his personality, yet also underscored what he viewed as his
continued role of teacher, one of his assignments when in the
military.

On a personal level, Chávez served as the embodiment
of the changes that occurred over the last two decades. His

own life story mirrored that of many Venezuelans previously marginalized from the national discourse. He established a deep personal bond with important segments of society that transcended the role of a traditional political leader, becoming a conduit for their collective aspirations. Over the course of nineteen elections, supporters participated in the electoral process, and with the exception of the 2007 constitutional reform, lent their backing to the government, usually with double-digit margins.

What is the nature of the opposition in Venezuela?

It is impossible to paint all those who oppose the Chávez government with one brush. The Chávez government has critics on both the right and the far left and opposition to the president is not monolithic. The left critique of Chávez varies, centering variously on the slow pace of change, the persistence of patronage, corruption, a bureaucratic party apparatus, the lack of internal democracy, a hyper-presidentialism focused on Chávez and now Maduro, and the lack of space to openly debate issues. Others on the left are also critical of the government practice that creates obstacles for public employees or others to organize labor unions and negotiate contracts. The lack of importance given to trade unions and the absence of union leaders in the party apparatus continue to baffle many on the left. Finally, some argue that the social missions created to address pressing needs, though more expansive, parallel previous efforts and that the *consejos comunales* (community councils) do not directly challenge capitalist economic relations.

Despite the left's critiques, it is the conservative opposition to Chávez that tends to dominate the discourse and receive attention in the local and international media. Though it has expanded in recent years, the conservative opposition draws most of its support from the middle- and upper-class sectors of society as well as professional groups. The opposition operates with two audiences in mind: its supporters in Venezuela and its allies abroad, where they hope to isolate the government by labeling it as authoritarian, repressive, and undemocratic. By increasingly radicalizing their tactics, some in the opposition sought to assure internal cohesion, close ranks, and reduce the likelihood of negotiations that would permit the government to claim legitimacy and consolidate power. The conservative opposition covers a wide spectrum of issues that has changed somewhat over time. Initially opposed to the constitution of 1999, they now fully support the document and use it to defend their position. Unwilling to recognize the limited nature of the 1976 nationalization law, they have been critical of the changes to PdVSA, declaring that it amounts to a government takeover of the oil enterprise. They complain that PdVSA has not increased production capacity from three million to five million barrels a day as it proposed earlier. Critics also assert that the country is today more dependent on oil, pointing out that oil has increased as a percentage of Venezuela's exports under Chávez. However, they don't take into account that oil prices have increased more than sixfold since Chávez took office and as a result reflect a much bigger percentage of Venezuela's exports. Moreover they claim that the use of PdVSA profits to fund social programs reduces resources with which to modernize the enterprise and expand production. They railed against Chávez's leadership style, and during his first term in office some in the opposition tried to have him declared insane to invalidate his presidency. They repeatedly criticize the inclusion of the military in politics, the politicization of the judiciary, the concentration of authority in the presidency, and the lack of transparency in the allocation of government resources.

The opposition has also been critical of the government's multipolar foreign relations, which no longer prioritize interactions with what they call "natural allies"—a direct reference to diminished ties with the United States. Foreign policy initiatives such as Petro Caribe that offer oil to Caribbean and

Central American countries on long-term credit are regularly attacked, with conservatives claiming that their goal is simply to curry favor in the region. Some in the opposition have even been critical of efforts at regional integration in which Venezuela has played a leading role. In recent years, however, the success of initiatives such as CELAC and UNASUR and full membership in MERCOSUR, the South American common market, has muted some criticisms on this front.

Denunciations of the polarization that exist in society are constant—however they fail to note that both sides have sustained the tenor of the political debate. The dramatic rise in crime, which remains a serious issue, is also a source of criticism, yet neither side has offered a comprehensive plan to fully address the matter. The increasing political rhetoric over crime prevents an honest, wide-ranging national discussion of the factors, both historic and contemporary, that give rise to crime. Corruption, a long-term recurring issue in Venezuelan political culture, is also a common source of criticism, as is the charge that government policy has given rise to a new elite, what some call the *boli-burgueses*, a Bolivarian bourgeoisie that supposedly benefits from lucrative government contracts. Complaints over a decaying infrastructure are constant and no doubt have merit; however, they also fail to account for the many new projects undertaken in the past decade, including rapid transit and the expansion of roads and freeways.

Opposition sympathizers regularly circulate reports that government officials have secret million-dollar accounts in US or European banks, although they cite no evidence to support their allegations. Paradoxically, until his death they had never suggested that President Chávez himself had ensconced public funds. Both the right and the left are critical of a disorganized, and at times stifling bureaucracy that has squandered resources and not adequately supervised the distribution of goods, a long-term problem now exacerbated by the new flow of oil money into construction projects, the subsidy of dollars, and even social programs.

One of the issues most often raised by the opposition and reproduced in the foreign media is freedom of the press. The portrayal of a powerful state repressing the media fails to capture the far more complicated reality in Venezuela, however. Those who make the charge refuse to acknowledge that, except for Radio Caracas Television (RCTV), which publicly supported and promoted the military coup of 2002, the commercial media continues to operate freely and usually sides with the opposition. In 2006, citing RCTV's role in the coup, the government refused to renew its license to use the public airwaves. Complaints about the increased role of government-sponsored media abound, yet its viewership amounts to a small fraction of the audience, and the great majority of Venezuela continues to watch mainstream commercial television outlets and international programming offered by satellite and cable.

Many opposed to Chávez expressed a view of society that created a false distinction between an educated and enlightened opposition fighting to save the country and defend democracy and an uneducated multitude led by a charismatic yet unscrupulous popular leader who retained support by squandering government funds on his followers. Opposition forces also continue to cling to an obsolete national narrative that oil permitted Venezuela to reconcile differences, fairly distributing resources among diverse social classes while promoting the modernization of the country. This analysis fails to recognize that during his first campaign in 1998 Chávez drew support from all sectors of society, not just the poor, but also disenchanted segments of the middle class and even the business community.

In its struggle against the government, the conservative opposition claims the mantle of civic society, a euphemism for the educated, usually professional, middle and upper classes. Their allies in this epic struggle have included at different times an array of nongovernmental organizations (NGOs) that claimed to promote democratic participation, the commercial media, the upper echelon of the Catholic Church, traditional business sectors, the traditional labor federations, and support from international organizations. Based on the proposition that society is hopelessly fragmented, fear has become a central element of the opposition discourse. The mainstream media and a largely selective process of association regularly reinforced these views and heightened fears among opposition sectors.

What celebrations do Venezuelans commemorate?

Celebrations in Venezuela highlight the cultural dynamics that exist in a society that embodies indigenous, European, and African cultural traditions. The vibrant relationships that have evolved between these three cultures are evident in Venezuelan festivities. Beyond expressions of cultural syncretism, celebrations also underscore the continued strength of regional identities in the country. Events in Venezuela reveal people's personalities, regionalism, and cultural traditions, as well as the impact of patriotic ideologies, religious impulses, and modern commercial enterprises.

As in most countries, traditional political holidays in Venezuela are inspired by historical events that are incorporated into the national imaginary. Not surprisingly, the most important dates in the Venezuelan civic calendar are April 19, which commemorates the launching of the independence process by the Caracas town council, and the July 5, which celebrates independence from Spain. As the preeminent leader of the independence process, Simón Bolívar's birth on July 24 and his death on December 17 are also significant national holidays. The festivities that evoke the most popular fervor, however, are those that adhere to the Christian liturgical calendar and build on folk culture and traditions and have become incorporated into the nation's social fabric. These holidays include the Christmas season, where in some communities the *pesebre* (nativity scene) is still carefully assembled and publicly displayed. In many urban areas, however, this tradition has been losing ground to more western commercial practices that include the use of an ornamental Christmas tree and colorful lights to commemorate the holiday. Between Christmas and New Year's fireworks can be heard throughout the day and night signaling the beginning of a community or a family festivity. In other areas, it is also customary to create an effigy of an old man that is burned at midnight on December 31 to signal the end of the year.

January 6 marks the feast of the *Reyes Magos* (Wise Men) or the Epiphany, which previously used to rival Christmas as the principal gift-giving holiday in Venezuela. In several western states, residents observe the *paradura*, or the first public exhibition of the Christ figurine, in which a couple dressed as Joseph and Mary parade the statuette in a procession accompanied by music around their community. The *paradura* marks the official end of the Christmas season and is typically celebrated between late January and the middle of February.

Although other established Catholic celebrations, such as Carnival and Easter, still generate religious fervor, they have generally become incorporated into the broader Venezuelan social calendar. Carnival is a tradition celebrated in coastal communities; however, the most famous Venezuelan celebration takes place in the mining town of El Callao, in the state of Bolívar. The carnival at El Callao draws inspiration from the diverse communities, drawn by gold mining, that settled there during the 1850s, including significant numbers of Afro-Caribbean people from Martinique, Guadeloupe, Trinidad, and Guyana. In addition, El Callao attracted Venezuelans from throughout the country that mingled with the descendants of the indigenous people that originally inhabited the area. A distinctive feature of Carnival at El Callao is the role of the *madamas* (madams) who wear highly colorful stylized dresses that draw inspiration from attire worn by women in the Caribbean and West Africa. The *madamas* and their coterie dance to calypso music and sing in patois, a mixture of Spanish, English, and local colloquial terms. People wearing ornate masks depicting mythological devils, and others whose entire bodies are painted in black, are also a part of the processions. The celebrations at El Callao attract tourists from throughout Venezuela and the Caribbean.

The veneration of saints and virgins has over time become the subject of popular devotions. These festivals are typically organized by *cofradias* (fraternities), which include a foreman, various captains, a host of secondary officials, and novices being introduced to the ritual. The *cofradias* bring together a network of family, community, and businesses to raise funds and sustain their work. The relations between the *cofradia* and the Catholic Church vary; some work closely with Church authorities while others maintain a degree of autonomy. The members of the *cofradias* are responsible for staging the events, negotiating with Catholic and town authorities, preparing the saints for the procession and veneration, ensuring the attire participants will wear, as well as organizing the music and dances. Fireworks are a central part of the veneration and serve to publicize the activity to the community.

Festivals associated with the veneration of saints and virgins emphasize the syncretic belief systems prevalent in Venezuela, the product of Spanish, African, and indigenous folk traditions. The veneration of a saint reflects different intentions depending upon the site of worship, which are as varied as a temple in the interior of a house, a popular celebration organized as part of a town festival, or a formal activity held in a Catholic church. Every distinct region in Venezuela possesses a potent tradition of popular legends and myths unique to each area, drawn from human experiences, encounters with nature, and reflections on the unknown. Although the Catholic Church generally sanctions these activities, there are tensions between the practitioners of these popular rituals and Church officials who feel they have lost control over the ceremonies.

On Corpus Christi Day, one of the most heralded rituals in Venezuela takes place in the central states of Miranda, Aragua, and Carabobo, areas with a strong Afro-Venezuelan presence. The festival of the Diablos de San Francisco de Yares, or the Devils of San Francisco of Yares, in the state of Miranda has been recognized as a Cultural Heritage of Humanity by UNESCO. The *cofradias* in San Francisco organize elaborate processions and ceremonies, where most participants dress in colorful red and multicolor costumes that include an elaborate mask that symbolizes the devil. Practitioners also carry maracas, religious characters, and palm fronds. The pulsating beat of drums and, in some cases, the *cuatro* (typical Venezuelan four-string instrument) accompanies the procession. A host of altars that include saints and offerings of fruit and flowers are erected along the procession route. The attire worn also helps denote the town or community from which each group originates. As is typically the case, the elaborate masks with multiple horns highlight the status of the individual in the *cofradia* and the higher-ranking members lead the procession.

In western Venezuela, San Benito is celebrated beginning in the last days of December and continuing through the first week of January. Although first venerated in Palermo, Italy, San Benito is adored by two very different communities in Venezuela. The first are Afro-Venezuelans along the southeastern coast of Lake Maracaibo and the second are mixed-race Andean communities in Mérida and Trujillo. In communities such as Ceuta, Bobures, or Gibraltar along the Zulia lakeshore, where cacao production had once been important, Afro-Venezuelans are the principal organizers of the daylong festivities. Church bells and fireworks announce the beginning of the festival. To a rapid-fire cacophony of *chimbangueles*, cylindrical elongated drums meant to make distinct sounds, San Benito is paraded throughout the town, eventually resting in the altar of a local Catholic Church. High in the Venezuelan Andes, in the community of Mucuchies, a largely mestizo (mixed race) *cofradia* organizes the festivities of San Benito, and participants paint their faces black and wear colorful attire to take part in the festivities. Throughout the year, followers of San Benito, or *San Beniteros,* carry the saint in a niche through towns to the accompaniment of drums or a violin.

Marian apparitions are also the source of significant devotion and the occasion of major festivities. One study points to over five hundred celebrations of distinct virgins, some acclaimed by immigrant groups such the Spanish who venerated La Candelaria and the Portuguese who tend to be devotees of Fatima. As is the case with many Latin American nations, the Church designated the Virgin of Coromoto as the country's patron saint and she is venerated on September 8. Marian apparitions, such as the Virgin of Guadalupe in Mexico, that purportedly appear to indigenous people tend to be mixed race—however, Coromoto is light skinned. Her apparition account is similar to many others; she reveals herself to a Cospes indigenous leader in the plains area of the state of Portuguesa seeking his conversion and surrender to Spanish authorities. Her apparition site is distant from large urban areas, thus minimizing her impact. Seeking to legitimate his rule and manipulate nationalist sentiments, the military government of Pérez Jiménez and the Catholic hierarchy orchestrated Coromoto's elevation as the patron of Venezuela in 1952. Although she is the official patron saint of Venezuela, she shares the religious pantheon with many other more popular Marian apparitions rooted in regional and ethnic experiences.

The Church retains formal jurisdiction of Marian apparitions; however, the festivities associated with the Virgin Mary in Venezuela have also moved into the realm of popular expression of faith and culture. In western Venezuela, the Virgin of Chiquinquira (known locally as the *Chinita*) is the subject of popular devotion and *zulianos,* the people of the state of Zulia, celebrate her feast day on November 18. In the state of Lara, the *Virgin de la Divina Pastora* (Divine Shepherdess) draws hundreds of thousands to Barquisimeto, the capital of the state of Lara, on January 14. The festivity honoring *La Divina Pastora* is the second largest in Latin America, surpassed only by the Virgin of Guadalupe in Mexico. On the island of Margarita, *Nuestra Señora del Valle* (Our Lady of the Valley) is the patron of eastern Venezuela, and she is also venerated on September 8. The popularity of the Virgin del Valle throughout eastern Venezuela is attributable to migration by residents of Margarita to other areas of the country.

Popular faith traditions also proliferate in Venezuela. One of the most important is the devotion to José Gregorio Hernández, known as the people's doctor, who was originally from Isnotú in the state of Trujillo. As a doctor in Caracas, trained in Europe, Hernández is credited with providing health care to the poor and indigent. After his death, run over by a car in 1919, he gained prominence among multiple social sectors. On various occasions, the Church and even presidents have sought his canonization without success. Although his remains are interned in the church of the Candelaria in Caracas, his birthplace in Isnotú has become a popular site of pilgrimage for people who seek his intervention or return to pay homage. The Church's reluctance to canonize Hernández has further contributed to his status as the people's saint and the doctor of the poor and his cult has spread to other areas of the Caribbean. During his presidency, Chávez named a social mission that dealt with people with disabilities in honor of Hernández and declared his birthday on October 26 a day of veneration.

The other popular figure venerated by thousands of Venezuelans is María Lionza, whose veneration draws inspiration from African, Spanish, and indigenous beliefs, and who is typically depicted atop a tapir. There are multiple origin accounts associated with the presence of María Lionza in Sorte, in the central state of Yaracuy. They share in common her supernatural powers and her role as protector of the rainforest, the streams, and the animals that inhabit the lush region. Unlike other beliefs, María Lionza does not have a relation with the Church, although at times she is conflated with the Virgin of Coromoto and depicted alongside José Gregorio Hernández and even Pedro Camejo (Negro Primero), an Afro-Venezuelan who fought for independence and died in the Battle of Carabobo. She is also closely associated with Yoruba deities and is often represented as part of a court that includes a largely anonymous Afro-Venezuelan named Negro Felipe and Guacaipuro, an indigenous *cacique* that fought the Spaniards. Not surprisingly these three figures incorporate the dominant ethnic and racial groups prevalent in Venezuela. The use of mediums in the cult of María Lionza underscores its similarity to Cuban Santeria. Typically people seeking relief from some malady or illness visit her shrine in Yaracuy and are attended by a medium that purports to communicate with María Lionza. The belief in María Lionza has spread to urban areas where people also gather to request her intervention. A statue of María Lionza sitting atop a tapir while lifting a female pelvis resides in the middle of the Francisco Fajardo freeway in front of the campus of the Universidad Central de Venezuela (Central University of Venezuela). Belief in María Lionza has spread throughout Venezuela, reaching into the Caribbean, and salsa artist Rubén Blades performs a song that popularizes her exploits.

Is baseball the most popular sport in Venezuela?

On the surface, with so many Venezuelans playing in the American major leagues, it may seem to people in the United States that the only sport that matters in the country is baseball. However, Venezuelans of all ages and backgrounds are involved in sports and games other than baseball. At the 2012 Olympics in London, Venezuelan Rubén Limardo won a gold medal in épée (fencing); Magnum Martínez was awarded a gold medal in the master's category by the International Surfing Association (2012); and Milka Duno, who has raced at Indianapolis and Daytona, is one of the most successful women drivers in the world. Sports in Venezuela reflect the country's diverse heritage and social complexity.

During the late colonial period, and into the nineteenth century, sports in Venezuela drew inspiration from Spanish traditions. Adapted to Venezuela by the *llaneros* (plainsmen), horse racing, bullfighting, and rodeo activities that include the *coleada de toros* (bull throwing) represent some of the most common forms of early public entertainment. In rural areas cockfighting still retains some devotees although it has diminished significantly in recent years. Horse racing remains popular in Venezuela and many major cities have racetracks. Since the late 1940s, aficionados have wagered on the races anywhere in the country through a national system of betting outlets where prizes are awarded to those who picked between five and six winners. Radio, and later television, broadcast Sunday afternoon races to the entire country. *La Rinconada*, an ultra modern racetrack, opened in Caracas in 1959, hosting national derbies such as the Simón Bolívar Classic and international competitions such as the *Clásico del Caribe* (Caribbean Classic). Venezuelan jockeys, such as Ramón Domínguez and others, compete in the United States and have won numerous awards. In 1971, Cañonero II, a Venezuela entry bought for $1,200, ridden by Gustavo Avila, won the Kentucky Derby and the Preakness. Due to an injury, the horse finished fourth in the Belmont stakes, thus being unable to win the coveted Triple Crown; nonetheless Cañonero's role as an underdog earned him the nickname of the "people's horse" among racing fans in the United States.[1] Although it no longer garners the passion it once did, professional horse racing still draws fans in Venezuela and the *coleadas de toros* are still held in cattle-producing states.

Some Venezuelans are also avid fans of *bolas criollas*, a game played on a rectangular dirt court (typically 25 by 15 meters) with round balls that weigh a little over a kilo. Although it resembles *bocce*, enthusiasts claim that the game is uniquely Venezuelan, since it is played with different weight balls and the court has different dimensions. The origins of *bolas criollas* in the country remain in doubt. Some suggest that a Spanish priest introduced the game during the colonial period as a form of entertainment for slaves. Despite its uncertain origins, the game remains popular; many communities have courts where people of various ages play the game. Since 1956, the *Federación Venezolana de Bolas Criollas* (Venezuelan Federation) sponsors a national championship that includes people of all ages and genders.

Venezuelans play, and avidly follow, a wide variety of western-inspired sports, including professional baseball, basketball, and soccer leagues. At the amateur level in nearly every sport, there are local and regional leagues and a significant number of men and women participate in sports-related activities. Venezuelans have won medals at Latin American and international championships in track and field, martial arts, boxing, weightlifting, fencing, cycling, softball, and youth soccer as well as volleyball. The US oil companies that operated in Venezuela sponsored regional and national championships in a wide variety of sports and heralded the accomplishment of their star employees in the local press. In 1949, the military government created a National Sports Institute to promote athletic activity. The Chávez government created a cabinet level Ministry of Sports in 2006 that encourages sports activities and provides financing to various leagues and regional bodies.

It is in baseball that Venezuela has established its strongest reputation with over eighty players in the US major leagues. Venezuelan teams have participated in the *Serie del Caribe* (Caribbean Series) founded in 1949, the premier Latin American baseball tournament that includes Mexico, Puerto Rico, and the Dominican Republic. Venezuelan teams have also played in the World Baseball Classic since its inaugural game in 2006. Venezuelan youth regularly compete in the Little League World Series, winning championships in 1994 and 2000.

The roots of baseball in Venezuela can be traced to 1895, when the Caracas Baseball Club (CBC) was formed in the capital by Venezuelans who had traveled to the United States and by immigrants from the Caribbean. Initially the cost of the equipment and the fields needed to play the game meant that most players were middle class Venezuelans and a handful of foreigners, including several from the United States and Cuba. With no other competition, the CBC created two squads and started public play in May of 1895, drawing over two-thousand spectators. By early 1900 the game had spread to several cities in the interior, and by 1902 a newspaper began to promote the game. That same year, the CBC team played against the sailors from a US Navy gunboat that was docked at the port of La Guaira, which serves Caracas. By the late 1920s baseball had begun to sink roots in Venezuela; a league formed, and intercity rivalries began to take shape. Venezuela was victorious in the Amateur World Series held in Cuba in 1941, where pitcher Daniel Canónico won five games. The series was broadcast by radio throughout Venezuela and helped popularize the game; throngs turned out to receive the returning champions, who became known as the Heroes of 1941.

The presence of US oil companies and their efforts to encourage what they considered "sound practices" among their employees led them to promote sports, especially the game of baseball. Companies such as Creole Petroleum Corporation, a subsidiary of Standard Oil Company of New Jersey, employed sports directors, built playing fields, purchased equipment, and promoted baseball and other sports among its employees. Every major oil camp in Venezuela had a baseball field and workers were encouraged to play the game, helping to further popularize the sport within Venezuela.

In 1939, pitcher Alejandro Carrasquel became the first Venezuelan to play in the US major leagues with the Washington Senators of the American League. His nephew Alfonso "Chico" Carrasquel was subsequently signed as a shortstop in 1948 by the Brooklyn Dodgers (he later played for the Chicago White Sox) becoming in 1951 one of the first two Latino players selected to play in the All-Star Game. In 1956, Luis Aparicio replaced Chico Carrasquel as the White Sox's shortstop, winning the Rookie of the Year award for his performance. In 1984 he became the first Venezuelan player inducted into the Baseball Hall of Fame. Since the 1960s an ever-increasing stream of Venezuelan players, especially infielders, have been signed by US professional teams, including the likes of David Concepción, Andres Galarraga, Wilson Álvarez, Johan Santana, Omar Vizquel, Bobby Abreu, Marco Scutaro, Ozzie Guillen, Magglio Ordoñez, Pablo Sandoval, and Miguel Cabrera. US Major League Baseball is regularly transmitted by television and radio and fans avidly follow the game as well as the performance of Venezuelan players.

Baseball has become the de facto national sport of Venezuela and avid fans can root for the *Leones* (Lions) of Caracas, the *Magallanes* (Mariners) of Maracay, the *Cardenales* (Cardinals) of Lara, the *Tigres* (Tigers) of Aragua, or the *Aguilas* (Eagles) of Zulia. Though it may have its roots in the United States, baseball in Venezuela, as is the case throughout the Caribbean, has become thoroughly Latinized. One US player in Venezuela remarked on the passion with which fans follow the competition, claiming the game felt like a match between gladiators. Nonetheless, Americans manage many of the teams, and US players often travel to Venezuela to play winter ball and hone their skills. Earlier, Negro League teams also travelled to Venezuela. In the winter of 1945, Jackie Robinson accompanied a black All-Star team and played in Venezuela. Venezuelan league play typically starts in early October so as not to conflict with the regular season of the US major leagues—in which many professional Venezuelans play—and the regular season consists of sixty-three games concluding at the end of December. It is followed by a league championship, known locally as the Round Robin, where five teams play each other in rotation. The winner of the championship typically represents Venezuela in the *Serie del Caribe*, and the World Baseball Classic.

Basketball also grew out of contact with foreigners in western Venezuela and efforts by sports clubs in Caracas, although it did not expand as quickly as baseball. By 1929, Caracas had sufficient teams to stage an amateur basketball tournament that included games by both men and women. The game continued to grow in popularity through the 1940s, and since 1992 Venezuela has had a professional basketball league (*Liga Profesional de Baloncesto*—LPB) with ten teams that play for a national championship. Several Venezuelans have played in the National Basketball Association (NBA) including Oscar Torres, Carl Herrera, and Greivis Vásquez. In 2014, Venezuela defeated Brazil, winning the South American Basketball Championship.

Unlike baseball and basketball, European immigrants, mostly from Italy or Spain, tended to dominate soccer in Venezuela. After several failed attempts, by 1926 play was organized under the auspices of a formal soccer federation. Despite its popularity in South America, the game never gained the mass following that baseball enjoyed. Forced to play against South America's best teams, Venezuela seldom advanced in regional competition.

In past decades, however, Venezuela has acquired a reputation as an important soccer competitor, reaching the finals in Latin American championships and defeating some of South America's most storied teams. PdVSA, the national oil company, has funded the training facilities for the national team, the *Vinotinto* (red wine), as well as covering other expenses. The Vinotinto now has legions of followers in the country and is beginning to reach levels of popularity previously reserved for baseball. In preparation for the 2007 Copa America (America's Cup), South America's soccer championship, being held in Venezuela for the first time, the government built a network of regional stadiums that have subsequently been used by local soccer clubs expanding its reach in the population.

Why do beauty pageants play such a large role in Venezuela?

The historical success of the Miss Venezuela pageant and accompanying media spectacle over what constitutes universal beauty demonstrates the extent to which some conditions in Venezuela have remained unchanged despite the election of Hugo Chávez. Amid political change, heightened polarization, protest, and counter-protest, many Venezuelans continue to closely follow the Miss Venezuela pageant. For some, the exaltation of beauty has penetrated the national consciousness, and is exhibited in attitudes, sensibilities, and cultural practices that shape the body images of both men and women. Venezuela drew international attention when its contestants Dayana Mendoza and Stefania Fernández won consecutive Miss Universe titles in 2008 and 2009 respectively. In 2013, Miss Venezuela Gabriela Isler was crowned Miss Universe. Venezuela currently holds seven Miss Universe, six Miss World, and several other beauty titles. Between 1980 and the early 2000s Venezuelan contestants were among the finalists in most Miss Universe and Miss World competitions. The contemporary Miss Venezuela beauty pageant dates from 1952, when Sofía Silva Inserri travelled to Long Beach to represent her country, beginning a process that has produced a steady stream of beauty queens. In 1955, Susana Lluijm won Venezuela's first Miss World crown.

The success of Miss Venezuela in international beauty pageants and the expansive media campaign that it generates have served to transform female beauty into a national obsession. Miss Venezuela contestants are typically promoted as ambassadors of the country, standard-bearers of the nation and its culture. Indeed, success at pageants earned Venezuela a sense of recognition and a marketable niche that rises to the level of oil and baseball. In fact, after several victories in international contests, in 1987 the newspaper *El Nacional* suggested that Venezuela would now be known for something other than oil. The promoters of the pageant sought to create the appearance that Venezuela now exported beauty, not simply oil. The lack of another recognizable export either in sports, culture, or music heightened the pageants' importance as a symbol of Venezuela. For many Venezuelans the beauty pageants became conflated as a symbol of nationality displacing more traditional indicators of identity. Success at pageants has allowed the country to achieve an international distinction that affirms its obsession with body image, youthful physical appearance, and the public display of sexuality.

Thousands of young girls eagerly participate in the cycle of pageants that take place every year with the hope of being selected. Venezuela is among the countries with the highest number of beauty pageants in the world. A select number of the winning contestants and finalists have leveraged their status to become news broadcasters, models, businesswomen, and in the case of Irene Sáez Conde, have delved into politics. For many young women, even if they do not win the coveted crown, the pageant is promoted as an opportunity to improve their social standing and gain access to a world that otherwise would elude them.

Since 1981, the pageant has been owned by the Cisneros organization. It also owns Venevisión, the television company that transmits the spectacle. At many levels the Miss Venezuela pageant resembles an integrated beauty conglomerate that generates lucrative profits for its promoters who license the name, attract corporate sponsors and sell its products. The Cisneros organization, for example, also owns or distributes a wide assortment of personal care and beauty products that are often featured on the pageant. Since the ascendancy of Osmel Sousa, a Cuban-born fashion sketch artist, as president of the Miss Venezuela organization in 1981, the group increasingly has been described as a "house of dolls" where beauty is carefully and skillfully sculpted. Rather than simply accept contestants as they are selected by regional or state pageants, the organization instead is methodical in its selection of participants. Sousa often travels to regional contests to supervise events; at times he personally selects candidates that he deems competitive, even if the candidate has not emerged victorious in the local event. The selected women are brought to the Miss Venezuela facility in Caracas where Sousa and a team of orthodontic and plastic surgeons evaluate them and determine the candidate's potential and the procedures they must undergo to continue in the screening process. In addition, the candidates endure rigorous training that includes posture, fashion, cosmetics, speech, diet, exercise, and public conduct.

The Miss Venezuela organization and Sousa as its president openly favor a Western European aesthetic, preferring women who are tall, slender, and typically white or very light skinned. Even contestants who may appear to have a mixed race background, with only slightly darker skin, typically possess normative European body and facial features. The preference for a preconceived body type tends to produce certain similarities between candidates from one year to the next. In media interviews Sousa has openly admitted that he does not consider Afro-Venezuelan women to be attractive, promoting a model of female beauty that largely excludes women of color, who represent the majority of the female population. In a country where beauty has become an obsession, the preponderance of slender, light skinned contestants that are regularly featured in the media reaffirms a dominant white aesthetic and female body type that sanctions existing power and gender relations.

The Miss Venezuela organization also conflates accomplishment on the runway with women's rights, suggesting that the success of the beauty queens grants women new power. Whereas this may be true for a select number of women who fit the pageants' specific criteria of beauty, the majority of women in Venezuela are left aspiring to a body and racial form that is largely unattainable. When Alicia Machado, Miss Venezuela (1995) and Miss Universe (1996), gained a few extra pounds (she claimed to have eaten too many *arepas* or corn cakes), the Venezuelan press reported on her efforts to lose weight. Regardless of their resources or socioeconomic situation, many women nonetheless continue to strive for this image, sustaining a medical, cosmetic, and personal care industry that profits from the beauty obsession. Venezuelan women and men, even those in the lower socioeconomic sectors, spend a significant amount of their personal income on these products.

The actual Miss Venezuela pageant is a massive media spectacle transmitted live on Venevisión. The event is rebroadcast throughout Latin America and is transmitted in the United States by Spanish-language television. The program typically extends upwards of four hours and always draws the lion's share of the television audience when it is transmitted. The event resembles a mixture of a pageant and variety show, featuring popular hosts, internationally known musical performers, artists, and an assortment of former beauty queens. Despite the selection process, in the end the candidates represent specific states and regionalist sentiments quickly surface. Although social movements that represent women and Afro-Venezuelans have often criticized artificial constructions of beauty, the pageant continues to enjoy popular support in contemporary Venezuela. Throughout Latin America and elsewhere, Venezuela continues to be identified with the success of its beauty pageant and its ability to win international titles.

How did telenovelas (soap operas) become so important in Venezuela?

By the middle of the twentieth century, advances in mass communication influenced popular culture. Commercial television first appeared in Venezuela in 1953, and by the early 1960s several channels competed to attract viewers. The US oil companies were among the first to use the medium to highlight their connection to the country, sponsoring a popular news program and variety shows. For those without monitors, viewing television became a social affair as neighbors congregated at homes that had a set and collectively watched a new genre known as *telenovelas* (soap operas). In Venezuela, unlike the United States, *telenovelas* dominated prime time.

Venezuelans became engrossed with *telenovelas*. One of the most popular, *El derecho de nacer* (The Right To Be Born), originally a Cuban radio soap (1948) and a Mexican film (1952) set in Havana, was remade and transmitted on Radio Caracas Television (RCTV), beginning in 1965 and lasting over two years. Venezuelan *telenovelas* tend to follow a predictable script, playing to themes of forbidden love, individual sacrifice, and personal redemption and hoping to attract an audience for whom these issues reflect their own unfulfilled aspirations. *El derecho de nacer* centered on a young doctor, whose birth was the result of an affair between the daughter of an elite family preoccupied with their status and a married man. The domineering family patriarch, don Rafael, first tried to have the fetus aborted; failing to find a doctor willing to perform the procedure, he ordered the child killed at birth. Rather than permit his death, the family's black nanny (played in blackface) took the boy to her home and raised him as her own child. While the distraught birth mother became a nun, the young man grew up to be a doctor who eventually saved the life of the grandfather that had ordered his death.

Playing on the success of the telenovela, the Billo's Caracas Boys, the country's leading orchestra, featured a song that included the despised patriarch don Rafael and the hero, Doctor Albertico Luna. The ability of the young doctor to reconcile the differences between his white elite family and the black mother who raised him spoke to the challenges Venezuelan society faced as it transitioned from a dictatorship to a new democracy. It also spoke to prevailing racial and social differences and the emerging middle class represented by the young doctor who overcame adversity to find happiness and a new social status. By the 1980s, *telenovelas* became a leading Venezuelan export to other countries in

Latin America and to Spanish-speaking audiences in the United States.

In the 1990s, hoping to capitalize on the social and economic crisis the country experienced, one television station promoted a new reality-based *telenovela*. *Por estas calles* (On These Streets) made its debut in 1992 and incorporated events that expressed Venezuela's new social reality, highlighting conditions in the barrios, police abuse, charges of corruption, and increased violence. Unlike many *telenovelas* that run for six months, *Por estas calles* ran for almost two years. Recent efforts by the government to promote its own social reality-based soap-operas have not taken root, and most viewers continue to prefer the traditional *telenovelas*.

What is the Sistema?

El Sistema refers to the program that introduces Euro-classical music and instruments to underserved children. The *Sistema*, known officially as the Fundación Musical Simón Bolívar (Simon Bolivar Musical Foundation), traces its roots to the work of José Antonio Abreu who, along with several colleagues, in 1975 initiated a program that brought together underprivileged youth to engage with Euro-classical music. What began with only a handful of youngsters had grown by April of that year to over one hundred participants and the National Symphonic Youth Orchestra held its first concert. The orchestra's slogan, coined in 1976—"Tocar y Luchar" (Play and Struggle)—summarizes the musical and also the social mission embodied in the collective effort of its young musicians to overcome adversity and promote musical excellence.

Beyond the immediate goal of musical proficiency in the Euro-classical tradition, the program instills children with discipline, social values, collective action, and determination, and builds a sense of pride in them and their community, allowing them to dream beyond their own personal circumstances. The lack of alternatives within Venezuela's poor

and working-class communities is revealed when many participants in the *Sistema* refer to the program as their second
family and a refuge of community and peace within their
violence-plagued neighborhoods. The government created a foundation in 1979 to support the work of the Youth
Orchestra, and Mr. Abreu secured finances when he was
Minister of Culture (1989–1993) under the second presidency
of Carlos Andres Pérez. However, funding was not consistent
and the *Sistema* continued to rely on sporadic corporate and
public funds to expand its outreach throughout the country.
The Chávez government dramatically increased funding for
the program, permitting it to greatly expand its influence
throughout Venezuela and attain an international profile.
Wearing their signature jackets representing the colors of the
Venezuelan flag, the top performers in the Sistema group tour
as part of the Youth Symphony and have thrilled audiences
around the world. The program currently touches the lives
of over 400,000 youth from lower socioeconomic sectors of
society who participate in a network of over ninety centers
that train infants, pre-teenagers, and teenagers to participate
in orchestras as well as choirs. The musical program has produced world-renowned musicians and musical directors, and
generated international interest in creating a similar model in
other parts of Latin America and elsewhere.

Gustavo Dudamel, the current musical director of the Simón
Bolívar Symphony Orchestra of Venezuela and the Los Angeles
Philharmonic, has undoubtedly become the international face
and virtual ambassador of the *Sistema*. Born in Barquisimeto
in western Venezuela in 1981 to a lower-middle-class family, he took up the violin at an early age, attended the same
musical academy as Mr. Abreu, and began to study conducting. Already exposed to music by his parents, the *Sistema* provided the structure, guidance and the broader environment
he needed to fully develop as a musician and eventually a
conductor. Winning the Gustav Mahler conducting prize in
Germany in 2004 brought him further international attention

and spotlighted the work of the *Sistema*. Inspired by the princi-
ples of the Venezuelan *Sistema*, the Los Angeles Philharmonic
has launched the Youth Orchestra of Los Angeles (YOLA),
which incorporates underrepresented students from throughout the city. Many music educators in the United States and
elsewhere point to the obvious social benefits as exemplified
by the *Sistema* to argue against the opposite direction taken in
their own countries, where funding cuts to education elimi-
nate music from the school curriculum.

Have conditions for Venezuelans improved significantly in the last decade?

During the late 1980s and the early 1990s poverty and levels of inequality increased dramatically in Venezuela.
According to the United Nations Economic Commission
on Latin America and the Caribbean (ECLAC), during
2002, poverty gripped 48.6 percent of the population, with
twenty-two percent living under conditions considered des-
titute. By 2010, according to ECLAC, poverty rates had fallen
to 27.8 percent, as extreme poverty declined to 10.7 percent.
The Venezuelan National Institute of Statistics (Instituto
Nacional de Estadísticas—INE) maintains that by 2011 poverty had fallen to 27.4 percent and extreme poverty to seven
percent. These indicators for poverty are based primarily on
income, which by itself represents a major change. The actual
conditions of the poorest citizens are even more improved
when one factors in the introduction of publicly funded
social programs that provide access to free or subsidized
health services, housing, food, and education previously
inaccessible to disadvantaged sectors of society. A significant
rise in consumption was also evident during the last decade,
even as the population increased from twenty-three million
in 2001 to nearly thirty million by 2014. Although it would
be hard to discern from mainstream news reports, a 2012
Gallup poll found that Venezuela ranked among the top five

of countries whose population had the most positive emotions in the course of a day.

The Chávez-era policy of public social investment, much of it channeled through a series of programs known as *misiones* (missions), has had a significant impact on the lives of millions of people in Venezuela. The missions have been funded with the profits generated from PdVSA, and the oil company is an important component of the social programs, assuming operational responsibility for several of them. In fact, the revenue the government allocates for social spending has increased dramatically in the last decade, upwards of sixty percent according to some estimates.

The number of missions has increased significantly to over twenty-five different programs, addressing health, literacy, education, sports, identity, land reform, senior citizens, the indigenous, culture, music, children, pensions, and energy, among others. The opposition claimed that the launching of the social missions in 2003 was timed to coincide with the hard fought 2004 recall election, which Chávez eventually won. In reality, most missions came later, and more decisive reasons explain their appearance. First, given the tremendous dominance of the oil industry over the nation's finances, such an expensive proposition would not have been viable until the defeat of the *paro nacional* that allowed the government to assert real control over PdVSA. Second, the mobilization and ensuing radicalization of the popular classes as a result of the coup and the *paro* increased pressures on the state to direct significant oil profits to those that helped the government overcome these challenges.

One of the first social missions, *Barrio Adentro* (Inside the Neighborhood), sought to deliver medical care, mostly primary and preventative, through a network of clinics in poor and working-class communities. Since the late 1980s, facing cuts in funding, cases of corruption, and a growing trend towards privatization, access to medical services had become increasingly prohibitive for poorer sectors of society. When ill, a significant percentage of the population self-prescribed medications—which became harder to obtain as prices soared—or sought non-Western remedies including *curanderos* (healers).

Facing resistance from the Venezuelan Medical Federation (VMF), the government contracted with Cuba to provide doctors to staff an emerging network of clinics. The Barrio Adentro program expanded gradually to include several thousand Cuban and Venezuelan doctors and a parallel number of health professionals and staff. At its height, it provided medical services in several thousand clinics and several hundred diagnostic centers. The ubiquitous Barrio Adentro clinics, typically red brick modules built at times with the assistance of the local community, served as the heart of the program.

For the poor sectors of society, with no previous access to healthcare, the existence of clinics in their own communities dramatically improved conditions of life. In effect, the program consisted of opening up hundreds of Urgent Care facilities, located in the poorest parts of the nation. In its first two years, the medical personnel were overrun with new patients from the vast number of families who for generations had never had enough money to see a regular doctor. After this initial rush, Barrio Adentro grew to include nutrition classes, exercise programs, and health maintenance previously unavailable to underprivileged sectors of society. The government expanded the program with a second and third phase aimed at providing more complex care and seeking to integrate services between clinics and hospitals. Eventually medical services included eye care through a program known as *Misión Milagros* (Miracle Mission) and dental services *Misión Sonrisa* (Mission Smile). The government exported aspects of Misión Milagros, offering eye care to other countries and outreach to the poor throughout Latin America.

Almost immediately, the opposition attacked the Barrio Adentro program. The VMF claimed medical personnel did not meet Venezuelan standards and offered substandard care, and took legal steps to block the implementation of the program. The mainstream press regularly reported on purported cases of medical negligence or even the defection of Cuban doctors to the United States. The Department of Homeland Security and the State Department launched the Cuban Medical Professional Parole Program (CMPPP) in 2006, offering defecting Cuban doctors from anywhere in Latin America asylum in the United States. According to a report released by Wikileaks in 2010, the United States frowned on Venezuela's attempts to export the program, fearing the destabilizing example an alternative socioeconomic model would provide among the poor of the region. Unable to directly criticize what amounted to a humanitarian mission, the Venezuelan opposition complained that funds expended abroad were being drained from projects needed in the country. Understandably, the government views Barrio Adentro as one of its signature missions, though it is not without shortcomings: services in some areas remain very uneven, and members of local *comunas* (communes) have complained about the lack of medicine for some of the more complicated illnesses.

The concept of the missions expanded into other areas, especially education. To address illiteracy the government launched *Misión Robinson* in 2003, taking the name used by nineteenth-century educator Simón Rodríguez when in exile. Using material developed initially in Cuba and used in other underdeveloped areas, the mission created a network of volunteer instructors who employed written and audiovisual materials to reach over one million people deemed illiterate. In 2010, UNESCO, the United Nations Educational, Scientific, and Cultural Organization, reported that 95.5 percent of adults and 98.5 percent of youth in Venezuela are now literate. It further reported that between 2003 and 2007 per capita spending on education for youth and adolescents increased by fifty-one percent. Access to a diverse array of relatively inexpensive publications has also increased. Works by Venezuelan and

Latin American writers are regularly sold below cost through a network of bookstores known as *Librerias del Sur* (Bookstores of the South) and at book fairs held regularly throughout the country.

One of the most significant efforts to improve education and diminish the digital divide was begun in 2008 when the government began to supply free laptops, known as *Canaima* (named after the Venezuelan Amazon region), to children in primary grades. Initially acquired in an agreement with the government of Portugal, the laptops aimed to advance access to technology and improve digital literacy among children in public elementary schools. Over two million children have been provided with the Canaima laptops, which employ open source software and are now being manufactured in the country.

Like Barrio Adentro, the Robinson program evolved beyond simply addressing literacy. It served as a bridge to other missions such as Misión Ribas, which provides courses to individuals that have not completed a secondary education, and Misión Sucre, which provides access to higher education at satellite campuses throughout the country. Misión Sucre also includes a pre-medical and medical component, *Medicina Integral Comunitaria*—MCI (Integrated Community Medicine), that seeks to train Venezuelan doctors and medical professionals to replace their Cuban counterparts and deliver services through Barrio Adentro.

To address the plight of thousands of high school graduates who failed to gain entrance into the traditional network of state-funded universities, in 2003 the government founded the *Universidades Bolivarianas de Venezuela*—UBV (Venezuelan Bolivarian Universities). The UBV has campuses in major cities such as Caracas and Maracaibo as well as in many states, providing access to over 400,000 students. Venezuela now has one of the highest rates of student enrollment in higher education in Latin America. The government's actions on this front appeared to have addressed the issue of access for thousands of students. However, it also increased expectations among graduates of the UBV, suggesting that, like their counterparts graduating from traditional public universities, they would be able to find remunerable full-time employment, a challenge under any condition and one that Venezuela continues to grapple with.

Controlled by the private sector and subject to market pressures, the price of food in Venezuela represents a significant percentage of the expenditure of many poorer and working people. During the year-end holidays in 2012, for example, Venezuelans reported spending upwards of forty-seven percent of their disposable resources on food. Taking a page out of the oil industry, where workers had access to company-operated commissaries to purchase food at fixed or subsidized rates, the government established a network of markets, known as *Mercal*, that provide basic foodstuffs at cost or at a reduced price. For most residents, the Mercal system provides significant savings over the private sector markets, and millions of Venezuelans have availed themselves of its services. In addition to the smaller fixed markets, Mercal also offers outdoor food fairs where consumers purchase a broader array of goods. In addition, the system has expanded to include a network of *Super Mercales*, combining the services of a regular mega-supermarket with the sale of electronics and clothing apparel. Needless to say, despite the initial success of these ambitious projects, they have not come without growing pains, and shortages are common.

During 2008, the government also launched PdVAL, a food distribution network sponsored by the oil company PdVSA to ensure access to food and to reduce hoarding, a constant complaint from customers. The system has faced many bottlenecks and inefficiency is still a factor. In 2010, tons of food was found rotting in a deposit in Puerto Cabello, one of the country's principal ports. Despite the fact that the country now produces more internally, scarcity of basic products remains a recurring issue. The presence of products from Brazil, Uruguay, Argentina, and other countries in South America, as well as electronic merchandise from China, reflects the diversity of trading partners with which Venezuela now interacts.

The *Misión Identidad* (Identity Mission) proved especially important since it sought to ensure that all citizens had access to *cédula*, a national identification card established in 1942. The card is required for any transactions with either the government or the private sector. The US oil companies operating in Venezuela were strong advocates of the identification card since it allowed them to better track their employees. Historically, most Venezuelans resented the bureaucratic delays at the national identification office and some had never obtained or renewed their cards, leaving them without an official identity and making them invisible to the state. Many immigrants, especially those from neighboring Colombia, had also been denied *cédulas*. Streamlining this process and creating mobile offices that traveled into communities facilitated the incorporation of thousands of individuals who had previously existed on the margins of society without proper identification.

Beyond the formal missions, there has been a cultural explosion in public art, street theaters, literary production, and community media, including radio, television and film. There has been a significant expansion in publicly produced media, with over two hundred new outlets, and many more print and digital venues. This growth permits neighborhoods and communities to produce and broadcast alternatives to what is transmitted on the commercial and government-controlled media. Stations such as *Radio Perola* (Radio Pots and Pans), which transmits from Caricuao, and Radio Negro Primero from the Sarría neighborhood serve to empower neighborhoods to tackle problems in their communities ranging from trash collection to addressing crime or even criticizing the government.

Under the auspices of the *Centro Nacional Autónomo de Cinematografía*—CNAC (Autonomous National Center for Cinematography) and the government-run *Villa del Cine* (Film

Villa), independent Venezuelan film production and distribution has also received a significant boost. Many of the films produced grapple with historical subjects, including those on the independence leader Francisco Miranda (2007), and *Días de Poder* (2011) (Days of Power), depicting life at the end of the Pérez Jiménez dictatorship. More traditional subject matter is encountered in films like the popular *Habana Eva* (2010) about a love triangle involving a young idealistic Cuban seamstress forced to choose between the love of two men, one Cuban and one Venezuelan.

One of the newer social programs is *Misíon Vivienda* (Housing Mission), which seeks to address the housing shortage that directly touches the lives of thousands of Venezuelans. As part of the mission, the government initiated a census of existing dwellings, which the opposition condemned as a pretext for confiscating people's unused dwellings. Sectors of the opposition actively campaigned against the census, and many refused to participate and register their residences.

The housing program is multifaceted and includes government-constructed projects where homes are sold to families under long-term low interest rates of credit. Another component includes providing construction materials to community collectives who then assume responsibility for building their own residences. The opposition claimed that the housing program, launched in 2011, represented yet another effort on the part of the Chávez administration to buy votes in preparation for the upcoming presidential election held on October 2012. For Venezuela's poor, many without housing or living in precarious *ranchos*, the criticisms fell on deaf ears. Rather the main criticisms from poorer residents has been the slow pace of building, the long waiting list, shoddy work, the lack of construction materials, and bureaucratic ineptness. Even so, expansion in building construction contributed in part to the 5.5 percent growth of the Venezuelan economy during 2012.

Despite the benefits it has provided, the mission system has not been institutionalized and it depends to a large extent on the budgetary priorities of the government in power. The missions are also driven largely by decisions made in Caracas; some critics claim there is a need for more decentralization and greater community input and local direction. The dramatic proliferation of missions also suggests duplication on many fronts. What is clear, however, is that the missions have served to improve the lives of average Venezuelans and contributed to an improved standard of living. The fact that the opposition candidate in the 2012 presidential elections committed to not dismantling all the missions and to establishing new ones underscores the importance of these programs to broad sectors of the population.

Why do politics remain so contentious in Venezuela?

Under any circumstance the process of political change can be unsettling for groups in society accustomed to a privileged status. Undoubtedly at the root of the political tensions in Venezuela are distinct visions of the country's past, its present, and its future course as a major oil-producing nation. The fact that the changes taking place in Venezuela have utilized the electoral arena to seek legitimacy heightens tensions as well. Since 1998, Venezuela has undergone nineteen separate contests to elect or reelect the president, governors, members of the national assembly, mayors, members of local city councils, and reforms to the constitution. Invariably, elections are cast as plebiscites on the president's policies, since any gain by the opposition serves as an opportunity to weaken the national government. Enjoying significant appeal among the population, Chávez also used this strategy, hoping to increase voter turnout by casting local and regional elections as referendums on his rule and the social policies introduced by the government. The process of multiple elections gives rise to a political climate in which political campaigning is constant and mobilizations by diverse sectors ongoing, drawing heightened media attention that undoubtedly contributes to the climate of polarization.

After boycotting the 2005 parliamentary elections, the opposition recognized the importance of participating in the electoral process. In 2006, conservative forces coalesced behind the governor of the populous, oil-producing state of Zulia, Manuel Rosales, although differences persisted in the antigovernment coalition. Rosales had previously been a member of AD and subsequently helped form a new party, *Un Nuevo Tiempo* (A New Time), in 2000. From the beginning Rosales faced several challenges. In 2002, he had signed the decree promulgated by Carmona during the coup, identifying him with the discredited forces that had previously ruled Venezuela.

In order to counter the social programs introduced by the government, Rosales's campaign proposed distributing a debit card to all citizens with which they could access their purported share of the oil wealth. Named *Fondo petrolero de los venezolanos* (Venezuelans Petroleum Fund), the campaign labeled the card *Mi Negra* (my black woman). Afro-Venezuelan supporters of the government charged that labeling the card *Mi Negra* and featuring a black woman in the commercials served as a not so subtle allusion to the role of Afro-Venezuelan nannies in the care of typically middle- and upper-class children. However, this was not Rosales' greatest problem. After the defeat of the recall effort in 2004, supporters of Chávez had become emboldened and the president enjoyed greater support, a fact that even the opposition pollsters recognized. Building from the experiences of the recall, government supporters formed the *Unidad de Batalla Electoral*—UBE (Electoral Units) to target sympathetic voters, and organized a "get-out-the-vote" campaign. In the end, Venezuelans reelected Chávez by 62.84 percent; Rosales captured 36.9 percent of the vote. As it had on occasions when Chávez appeared on the ballot, voter turnout reached over seventy percent.

As they had after 2004, the opposition initially fell into disarray amidst accusations over responsibility for the electoral defeat. In the wake of the nonrenewal of the license for RCTV and as the Chávez government proposed far-reaching constitutional reform in 2007, university students from private and even public universities emerged as the leading voice for the opposition, taking to the streets and dominating the message in the media. At first, the government appeared taken aback by the protests by students, traditionally a natural ally of progressive causes. However, as access to universities had increasingly been restricted and costs increased, the composition of the campuses had changed and the institutions of higher learning no longer reflected the intellectual and social trends of earlier decades. Nonetheless, within a few months dueling student organizations—those supporting the opposition and those supporting the government— emerged and joined the partisan political fray.

In 2007, after receiving input from the national assembly and various social movements, the Chávez government proposed to amend the constitution. The reforms introduced new socialist concepts to the constitution, reflecting Chávez's increasing reference to the concept of "21st century socialism." The more than sixty reforms institutionalized the role of communes, introduced the concept of collectively owned land, restructured the national territory, prohibited discrimination over a person's sexual orientation, openly recognized the contributions of Afro-Venezuelans and the indigenous, reduced the work week, added socialist humanism to the educational curriculum, and further protected PdVSA from privatization.

While challenging most provisions, the opposition focused on what they considered the central clauses in the constitutional reform: the recognition of various forms of property rights, including private and collective; an effort to extend the presidential term from six to seven years; and the indefinite reelection clause that permitted Chávez to stand for election again in 2012. With students taking the lead, the traditional opposition—the political parties, the high clergy of the Catholic Church and the media—rejected the reforms. In a very close election, with a high level of voter abstention, the opposition defeated the constitutional reforms with 50.7 percent voting No and 49.2 percent voting Yes. The defeat of the 2007 constitutional reforms represented the first time since 1998 that the government and its allies had suffered an electoral defeat. Chávez acknowledged the defeat, vowing to reconsider the reforms at a later date.

Constitutional reforms in Venezuela can be initiated by the president, a two-thirds vote of the national assembly, or by signed petitions representing fifteen percent of the population. A new constitutional reform that allowed all elected political officials, not just the president, to seek indefinite reelection emerged from the Chávez-controlled national assembly. Supporters of the proposal also turned in over four million signatures—more than enough to trigger an election. The opposition ardently opposed the proposed change, insisting that the new proposal represented an illegal effort to reintroduce reforms previously defeated in 2007. However, with several pro-opposition pollsters showing the proposal trailing, some opposition leaders expressed confidence that they could defeat the reform and deal the government an important blow, weakening its position. To rally their forces, opposition forces organized around a No coalition and the pro-government forces formed a Yes block. After an intense thirty-day campaign, with close to a seventy percent level of voter participation, 54.86 percent of Venezuelans approved the constitutional reform, creating the conditions for Chávez as well as opposition-elected officials to seek reelection in 2012 and beyond.

Having boycotted the parliamentary elections of 2005, the opposition opted to participate in the parliamentary elections of 2010. In preparation for this contest, they formed the *Mesa de la Unidad*—MUD (Unity Table) in January of 2009, which brought together the leading opposition parties. The opposition promoted the elections to the national assembly as a referendum on the Chávez government and a preview of the presidential elections scheduled for 2012. Although the opposition made important gains, winning sixty-four seats and closing the gap in the actual number of votes, the pro-Chávez forces retained ninety-eight seats in the assembly. The opposition claimed that the redistricting by the assembly prevented them from actually increasing their numbers. Ultimately, however, the stronger showing by the opposition denied the government the supermajority needed to promote major changes and increased gridlock on important issues.

The 2012 presidential elections represented the sixteenth electoral contest held since Chávez was first elected. Organized around the MUD, the opposition held a much-publicized primary with candidates Pablo Pérez, the governor of the state of Zulia; María Corina Machado, a member of the national assembly; and Henrique Capriles Radonski, the governor of the populous state of Miranda. A descendant of one of Venezuela's wealthier families, Capriles Radonski studied law before entering politics as a candidate for the COPEI, the Christian Democrats. He first ran as a candidate for the national assembly from Zulia even though he did not actually reside in the state. He helped launch the *Primero Justica* (Justice First) Party in 2000, and in 2008 became governor of the populous state of Miranda, which encompasses a significant portion of eastern Caracas. The favored candidate of the opposition, he easily won the 2012 primary, with a little over three million people participating.

With Capriles as their candidate, the opposition insisted they would defeat Chávez. An array of pro-opposition polls and dozens of media accounts in the Venezuelan and international press reinforced the notion that Chávez, running for a fourth time, appeared vulnerable. The fact that Chávez had undergone treatment for an undisclosed cancer in June of 2011 only heightened speculation among conservative forces of his

Figure 5 Launching the presidential campaign of 2012. Hugo Chávez is pictured with the top PSUV leadership.

impending defeat. Capriles presented himself as an energetic forty-year-old competing against a weakened and possibly ill political leader. Recognizing that he had to win over Chávez supporters to prevail, Capriles claimed to draw inspiration from Luiz Inacio "Lula" da Silva, the former moderate leftist president of Brazil. Moreover, unlike previous conservative candidates, he insisted he would not dismantle the Chávez-era social programs that had reduced poverty in Venezuela. The insistence on victory, even when other polls indicated a significant lead for Chávez (Figure 5), was intended to rally support among opposition forces that might be weary of yet another electoral defeat. It also served to influence coverage by the international media that was then reproduced in Venezuela. The local media regularly publishes reporting about Venezuela in the foreign press to validate their assertions and their sense of reality.

In the end, the election on October 12, 2012 produced a victory for Chávez, who garnered 55.1 percent of the vote to Capriles's 44.3 percent. Participation in the election was high, with over eighty percent of the electorate turning out to vote. Elections for governors on December 16, 2012, the first election in which Chávez did not personally campaign for candidates, produced a resounding victory for the *Partido Socialista Unificado de Venezuela*—PSUV (United Socialist Party of Venezuela) which won twenty of the twenty-three governorships. Capriles easily won reelection in the state of Miranda, where he actually drew a significant amount of support from the poorer sectors of the state.

What were the effects of Chávez's illness?

On December 8, 2012, during a nationally televised broadcast, Chávez announced that he would be returning to Cuba to undergo what amounted to a fourth cancer operation. He first revealed that he suffered from a form of undisclosed cancer in the pelvic area in June 2011. He underwent several surgeries and chemotherapy and claimed during the summer of 2012, as he prepared to run for the presidency, that he had been cured of cancer. Addressing his own mortality, he asked his followers to support his newly named vice president Nicolás Maduro in any future election if he became incapacitated and could not fulfill his term in office.

With Chávez receiving treatment in Cuba, and unable to be present for his inauguration on January 10, 2013, the opposition insisted that Venezuela confronted a constitutional crisis. The State Department and multiple editorials in leading US newspapers echoed the opposition's position. The Venezuelan Supreme Court ruled no crisis existed, since the reelection of Chávez implied an administrative continuity.

The opposition continued to question the government's legitimacy while insisting that deep divisions existed among the president's supporters, a view quickly echoed by the Venezuelan and international media. They painted a picture of fierce infighting between Maduro, the vice president, and Diosdado Cabello, the president of the national assembly who, like Chávez, emerged from within the ranks of the military. This purported division rested on the notion that Cabello represented a pragmatic, thus more conservative faction of "Chavismo." Maduro was typically depicted as an ideologue defending the more radical wing of the former president's party. The opposition also regularly accused Maduro of being a puppet of the Cubans. Beyond divisions, the opposition sought to have Chávez declared unfit to perform his duties to trigger a need for a new presidential election within thirty days. Although conservative leaders embarked on a tour of Latin America, the opposition proved unable to generate support in the region.

After a prolonged illness, President Hugo Chávez died on March 5, 2013. The president's death generated an outpouring of public grief and popular support never previously seen in Venezuela. Grieving crowds waited hours in scorching heat to view his body as it lay in state at Fuerte Tiuna. Authorities prolonged the viewing to accommodate the crowds and decreed seven days of national mourning. Representing his impact in international affairs, heads of state from throughout Latin America and other world leaders attended his memorial services. The United States sent an official delegation; the Reverend Jessie Jackson and actor Sean Penn also attended the memorial. Breaking with tradition, both Catholic and Protestant clergy participated in the prayer service. The Venezuelan Youth Philharmonic conducted by Gustavo Dudamel played "Gloria al Bravo Pueblo," the national anthem, and other popular *llanero* (plains) musicians performed. Authorities eventually placed Chávez in a mausoleum at *Cuartel de la Montaña* (Barracks of the Mountain), the site from where he launched the failed coup of 1992. His tomb has become a place of pilgrimage for many of his followers who regularly visit the site.

*Who is Nicolás Maduro and why was the April 14th election
so close?*

Nicolás Maduro was born in Caracas on November 23, 1962: in his youth he played baseball, performed on bass guitar in a rock band, and became a student organizer. He worked as a driver, subsequently assuming a leadership position in the trade unions that represented the Caracas bus and subway conductors. Along with his future wife Cilia Flores, an attorney, he joined the Chávez movement and became part of the effort to free him from jail. The couple also dabbled in eastern religions, becoming followers of Satya Sai Baba, and traveled to India in 2005. Flores also became the first woman to head the national assembly between 2006 and 2011. Maduro served as a member of the national assembly, a member of the constituent assembly that drafted the constitution, and subsequently assumed the role of Minister of Foreign Relations before being named Vice President. As foreign minister he became a proponent of the policy of regional integration and an important figure in normalizing the previously fractured relations with Colombia.

As vice president Nicolás Maduro assumed the position of president after Chavez's death. The opposition protested the move, insisting that the constitution required the president of the national assembly to assume the position. With the process of scheduling elections underway, the opposition continued to cast doubts on Maduro's legitimacy. Eventually the electoral council selected Sunday April 14, 2014 for the presidential election to replace Chávez.

Occurring five weeks after Chávez's death, the elections represented a significant challenge to the groups that supported the government. Coming on the heels of a very emotional period of national mourning, pro-Chávez forces confronted a well-organized and buoyed opposition. Foreign adversaries were also emboldened, including the Washington foreign policy establishment and conservative forces that saw Chávez's death as an opportunity to turn back the tide in Venezuela and eventually throughout Latin America.

The candidate of the PSUV and the *Polo Patriótico* (Patriotic Front, a coalition of left parties), Maduro had never run a national campaign. His only experience with electoral politics had been as a candidate to the national assembly for a district in Caracas, which he won. Since 2006 he had spent much of his time dealing with international affairs. Promising continuity, the Maduro campaign relied heavily on Chávez's image and his legacy to convey their message.

The five weeks between Chávez's death and the election gave the opposition time to make their argument and win over people unwilling to trust Maduro or those for whom the promise of change remained unfulfilled. In early February, with Chávez ill in Cuba, the government announced a devaluation of the bolivar from 4.3 to 6.3, increasing speculation and inflating the price of the dollar on the illegal parallel markets. An active speculative bubble had pushed the bolivar to record highs on the parallel market, reaching as high as a 70 to 1 ratio. Web pages operated outside of the country provided daily quotes of what they called *lechuga verde* (green lettuce) a not to subtle reference to the US dollar. Scarcity of basic products persisted, leading many to engage in frenzy-buying of basic products, further increasing shortages. The government alleged that merchants, as they had done in the past, were hoarding products, artificially generating shortages to affect the outcome of the election. Electrical blackouts in late March and early April affected Caracas and other states, highlighting persistent infrastructure problems.

In contrast to Maduro, the conservative candidate Henrique Capriles had twice run for governor of the state of Miranda, which he won, and once for president. In an effort to win over voters who had supported Chávez, but were critical of government inefficiency, spiraling inflation, and persistent food shortages, Capriles once again cast himself as a moderate, leading some to label his campaign "Chávez light." The transformation from conservative to moderate was aided by the national and international media, which described Capriles as a "centrists'" candidate. The Maduro campaign did not fully appreciate the challenge Capriles represented and the extent to which some sectors that had previously supported Chávez had grown disillusioned with the government.

With a high level of participation (over seventy-nine percent) the election of April 14, 2013 produced a narrow victory for Maduro. In the end the electoral council confirmed that Maduro had received 7,587,579 votes and Capriles 7,363,980—a difference of 1.49 percent. The results of the April 14 elections recast the political landscape. In every previous presidential election, Chávez had managed to win decisively, defeating opposition candidates in most cases by double digits. Immediately the opposition challenged the results of the election and refused to recognize the Maduro victory. Capriles called on his supporters to take to the streets. The ensuing protests became violent and several people perished. The United States also refused to recognize Maduro's election despite the fact that all the countries of Latin America, China, Russia, and some European states recognized the outcome. Maduro was sworn into office on April 19, 2013 at a ceremony attended by several Latin American heads of state. In the ensuing weeks, in an effort to demonstrate transparency and address opposition concerns, the electoral council conducted an audit of the electoral process confirming Maduro's victory. Despite the audit, the Venezuelan opposition and the United States refused to recognize the results of the election, hoping to delegitimize Maduro. Some in the opposition also formed a "birther" movement, asserting that Maduro was actually a Colombian, not Venezuelan. They filed a motion to have the election annulled for these reasons; the Supreme Court ruled against them.

What was the importance of municipal elections of December 2013?

On December 8, 2013, Venezuela held elections for 335 mayoralties and some three thousand municipal positions. The opposition had hoped to capitalize on the continued shortages of basic food products and skyrocketing inflation of over fifty percent to win the municipal elections. They cast the municipal elections as a plebiscite on the Maduro government and did an about-face, calling on their supporters to trust the national electoral council that they had vilified in the April 2013 presidential elections. Looking beyond the municipal elections, they hoped to defeat the PSUV and its allies and set the stage for a national recall election in 2016. Part of their tactics included efforts at promoting conditions of ungovernability in the months before the election, which resembled the hyperbole, though not the mobilizations, that occurred in the weeks preceding the 2002 coup. Claims that Maduro would be toppled by a military coup or forced to resign appeared frequently in the opposition media. Political commentators insisted that the PSUV was wracked by factionalism and had lost support among the population.

The Maduro government appeared slow to react to the opposition attacks. By early November a response took shape when the government announced that it would guarantee Christmas bonuses (*aguinaldos*) for state employees. Then on November 11, 2013, the government audited a large electronics firm, asserting that they charged exorbitant prices and compelling the company to dramatically reduce prices. Hundreds of people flocked to the store to purchase goods at regulated prices. The government contended that merchants bought merchandise with regulated dollars from the state and then set prices based on the value of the bolivar on the parallel market (upwards of seventy to the dollar) making exorbitant profits. Employing the government's consumer agency, the Maduro administration launched its counteroffensive to what it called an "economic war" and attempted to portray itself as the defender of the average consumer. In full view of the media, officials carried out inspections at dozens of retail stores and even threatened to set prices on Venezuelan's sky-rocketing real estate. The opposition decried the government's actions as an attack on free enterprise, contending that the policies would turn the populace against the government.

Compared to the narrow April 2013 presidential elections, on December 8 the PSUV and its allies won a significant victory, gaining or retaining control over seventy percent of may-oralties and municipalities in the country. Despite winning an important victory and gaining some breathing space, the gov-ernment proved unable to make inroads in the principal met-ropolitan areas such as Caracas or Maracaibo. The opposition held on to the four Caracas boroughs, including Sucre, home to the large working-class area of Petare. In Maracaibo, the second largest city, the opposition candidate Evelyn Rosales (wife of the former governor and presidential candidate) was reelected.

What caused the protests that erupted in February 2014?

On February 12th, Venezuelan Youth Day, some university students and traditional conservative opposition groups took to the streets in several major cities. In Caracas, protestors attacked a government building, burned cars, and damaged the entrance to a metro station. Subsequent protesters targeted medical facilities, transportation hubs, universities, and the regional offices of the electoral commission. The demonstra-tions extended for several days, and it quickly became obvi-ous that the principal purpose of the protests was once again to destabilize the government and seek the ouster of Maduro. Reports in some international media outlets gave the impres-sion that Venezuela faced an unprecedented crisis. Some accounts went so far as to compare the situation in Venezuela to the crisis in Ukraine or worse Syria, suggesting that the government would soon collapse. As is usually the case, however, events in Venezuela were more complicated than they first appeared.

Several factors drove the protests in the early months of 2014. Undoubtedly, the country faced serious problems: skyrocketing inflation, shortages of basic products, and the recurring issue of crime. However, the opposition leaders who directed the protests were also motivated by other factors. Venezuela does not have national elections scheduled during 2014, a rarity in the country's exceedingly active electoral cycle that has undergone nineteen elections since 1998. The earliest elections are not scheduled until December 2015, when voters go to the polls to elect members of the national assembly. The presidential recall provision of the constitution cannot be triggered until 2016. Unwilling to allow the Maduro government time to consolidate, and hoping to precipitate a crisis, some leaders of the conservative opposition, including Leopoldo López (a US-educated former mayor of Chacao, a borough of Caracas), María Corina Machado (a member of the national assembly), and others sought to mobilize forces and take to the streets. López and Machado organized under the banner of *La Salida* (The Exit), proposing the departure of Maduro. The protests also represented a direct challenge to the leadership of Henrique Capriles, the previous leader of the opposition.

A distinguishing feature of the 2014 protests was the fact that they primarily took place in middle- and upper-middle-class neighborhoods controlled by opposition mayors and did not spread to other urban areas. Working-class areas and poorer sectors of major cities did not participate in the protests, an issue that frustrated the opposition. Venezuela has over 335 municipalities and protests initially took place in less than eighteen, quickly dropping below that in a matter of weeks. The economy in areas beset by protests ground to a halt as merchants and business sectors complained that they could not stock supplies, aggravating shortages and increasing speculation. It is estimated that the current protests, and the damages they caused, have cost the country several billion dollars.

On multiple occasions, the police, and in some cases the military, have clashed with protestors. Over the course of several months, the number of killed has reached over forty, and violence took its toll on both protestors and supporters of the government. Some in the opposition targeted the military, and several soldiers and officers were killed. The opposition claimed that the government unleashed the military and state forces on protestors. The government ordered an investigation and several security personnel have been arrested for abuse of power. However, the reality is that the number of injured and dead would have been much higher had the military been instructed to senselessly attack the protestors.

The demonstrations proved unable to oust Maduro; however, they did reveal a deeply divided opposition, tangentially united only in their efforts to unseat the president. Each of the purported leaders of the *Salida* strategy, first López and subsequently Machado, sought to leverage the protests and emerge as the leading figure of the opposition. Authorities charged López with inciting violence, and at a very public media event, he turned himself in and awaits trial. After Machado sought to testify before the Organization of American States (OAS) as a delegate of the Panamanian government, she was stripped of her position in the national assembly. For his part, Capriles has largely been sidelined by the protests and his standing has fallen precipitously within the opposition.

Beginning in March 2014, the government launched its own initiative and convened a series of national peace conferences to address issues raised in the protests. During March 2014, the countries of UNASUR (Union of South American Nations) offered to broker a meeting between the Venezuelan government and the opposition forces. Earlier, a majority of Latin America countries blocked an effort spearheaded by Panama to have the OAS mediate the situation in Venezuela. The vote against action by the OAS underscores Washington's isolation in the region; the only countries voting for the resolution were Panama, Canada, and the United States. A delegation of UNASUR foreign ministers visited Venezuela and met with both the government and the opposition, agreeing to mediate dialogue between opposing sides. In early April 2014 they arranged a highly anticipated and nationally televised summit between the government and the opposition. After several meetings, by the middle of May the opposition decided to boycott the mediation meetings, citing the lack of results. By the summer of 2014, infighting between the conservative parties that comprise the MUD became public, and the leader of the umbrella organization resigned.

On the diplomatic front, there have been efforts to normalize relations between the United States and Venezuela. Despite not formally having ambassadors since 2010, in July of 2014, Venezuela and the United States exchanged *chargé d'affaires*, a step that most observers see as positive. Venezuela's promotion of Petro Caribe also drew the attention of US officials. Earlier in 2014, General John F. Kelly of the United States Southern Command expressed concern that the economies of the region might "collapse" if Venezuela curtailed the sale of oil through Petro-Caribe (oil sold on long-term credit) In the aftermath of such a decision, Kelly feared that the United States would face a potential wave of immigration from the Caribbean and Central America.

What is the Chávez legacy in Venezuela?

What will transpire in Venezuela in the foreseeable future is difficult to foretell. What is clear, however, is that the Chávez presidency marked an important watershed in the country's history and throughout Latin America. After having been ruled by military strongmen for most of the twentieth century, and the political parties of the Punto Fijo pact for nearly forty years, since 1998, through nineteen elections, Venezuelans have lent their support to the Bolívarian process initiated by Chávez.

Chávez's appeal among multiple sectors of Venezuelan society transcends the role of a traditional political figure. His humble origins, mixed-race background, and ability to communicate allowed him to connect with common citizens. However, to focus exclusively on the figure of Chávez fails to capture the levels of popular mobilization that sustained the government through periods of crisis and triumph.

Fueled by a legacy of social movements and community organizations, the levels of civic participation in Venezuela have increased dramatically in the last decade. Although not welcomed by all sectors, previously marginalized groups have become emboldened, assuming leadership in their communities and on the national political stage. Associations of Afro-Venezuelans, women, workers, the urban poor, and indigenous groups have begun to redefine concepts of citizenship and civic participation previously dominated by the middle and upper classes. The process of civic engagement extends to the opposition as well, which now feels it can no longer take for granted its status and feels obligated to defend its interests in society. Aside from the tensions that this process invariably generates, there is a new sense of identity in the country. What it means to be Venezuelan is being debated in neighborhood, homes, schools, and workplaces. Despite perceptions in the United States, Venezuelans are likely to rate the quality of their democracy very differently: On a scale of 1 (My country "is not democratic") to 10 (My country "is totally democratic") the average score for Venezuela is 7, the second highest in Latin America, trailing only Uruguay.[2]

Within Venezuela, the death of Chávez left a tremendous void within the social movements and political process he helped shape. Despite many advances, Venezuela faces multiple challenges, some driven by internal economic and political conditions, and others by changing international circumstances.

Chávez remained the singular figure that commanded respect and proved capable of drawing together the diverse political forces that represented the many faces of the Bolívarian movement. His death highlights the strengths, but also the limits, of an all-powerful, charismatic hyper-presidentialism expected to resolve issues, but whose omnipresence casts others in a secondary role. Nicolás Maduro, the current president, has the unenviable position of filling this void and continuing the Chávez legacy without the cultural capital or political authority of his predecessor. In the last year, dissonant voices on the left have become much more common.

The contemporary Venezuelan reality embodies multiple and at times seemingly contradictory social and economic experiences. The government's conception of twenty-first century socialism coexists alongside capitalist economics, a strong sense of individualism, and a highly consumer-oriented society defined by conspicuous consumption. As it promoted twenty-first century socialism, the government seldom addressed these inherent contradictions. On the one hand, many people actively participate in the work of community councils and social missions, while on the other they also function in a capitalist-oriented world in which consumption and the values it imposes continue to play a significant role in society. How these two approaches will be reconciled or if they continue to coexist in their current hybrid state will determine the character of Venezuela's social experiment.

After fifteen years in power, there is evidence of political fatigue, apparent in the bureaucratization and inefficiency in the delivery of existing services, including the much-heralded missions. Dependence on oil continues to create distortions in the economy, scarcity of basic products persists, multiple currency exchange rates are unsustainable, and inflation has skyrocketed. Pressure to expand housing services and access to basic consumer goods will persist as the population continues to dramatically increase, passing thirty million, over 90 percent of which resides in urban areas. The incorporation of new consumers will invariably increase expectations for continued access to goods and an improved standard of living. Although internal production has increased, the country still imports the lion's share of what it consumes. The dramatic reduction in poverty has not diminished inequality and crime continues to be a serious problem. Internationally, the expansion of oil production in the United States and a drop in the price of oil may present Venezuela with new challenges.

The serious problems that Venezuela confronts can only be addressed through a concerted process of national dialogue that involves all sectors. Venezuela, however, lacks a traditional political opposition willing to challenge the government and offer concrete alternatives or a distinct vision of the nation, while at the same time respecting the outcome of democratic elections. The absence of a democratic opposition creates serious problems for the country, generating a heightened confrontational political culture that impacts the discourse and policy choices of both the right and the left. The willingness of the right to rely on extraparliamentary tactics, as exemplified by the recent efforts to oust Maduro, underscores that they continue to view politics as an all-or-nothing scenario.

Venezuelans are discerning voters and will lend their support to those able to best address the very serious issues they confront. No matter what happens in Venezuela, it is unlikely that the country will return to the period that existed before the election of Hugo Chávez.

Notes

1. Allen Hetherington, "Cañonero II brought out the underdog in all of us," *New York Times*, December 6, 1981.

2. "Country Image and their Democracies," ("Imagen de los países y sus democracias,") Latinobarómetro Report, July 9, 2014, http://www.latinobarometro.org/latNewsShow.jsp.

SUGGESTED READING

Betancourt, Rómulo. *Venezuela, Oil and Politics*. Boston: Houghton and Mifflin, 1979.

Ciccariello Maher, George. *We Created Chávez: A People's History of the Venezuelan Revolution*. Durham, NC: Duke University Press, 2013.

Coronil, Fernando. *The Magical State: Nature, Money, and Modernity in Venezuela*. Chicago: University of Chicago Press, 1997.

Diaz, Arlene. *Female Citizens, Patriarchs, and the Law in Venezuela, 1786–1904*. Lincoln: University of Nebraska Press, 2004.

Ellner, Steve. *Rethinking Venezuelan Politics: Class, Conflict, and the Chávez Phenomenon*. Boulder, CO: Lynne Rienner, 2008.

Ewell, Judith. *Venezuela and the United States: From Monroe's Hemisphere to Petroleum's Empire*. Athens, GA: University of Georgia Press, 1996.

Fernandes, Sujatha. *Who Can Stop the Drums? Urban Social Movements in Chávez's Venezuela*. Durham, NC: Duke University Press, 2010.

Ferry, Robert J. *The Colonial Elite of Early Caracas: Formation and Crisis 1567–1767*. Berkeley: University of California Press, 1989.

Gallegos, Rómulo. *Doña Bárbara*. Translated by Robert Malloy. Chicago: University of Chicago Press, 2012.

Gates, Leslie. *Electing Chavez: The Business of Anti-Neoliberal Politics in Venezuela*. Pittsburgh, PA: University of Pittsburgh Press, 2010.

García Márquez, Gabriel. *The General and His Labyrinth*. Translated by Edith Grossman. New York: Vintage, 2003.

Guss, David. *The Festive State: Race, Ethnicity, and Nationalism as Cultural Performance*. Berkeley: University of California Press, 2001.

Hellinger, Dan, and Smilde David, eds. *Venezuela's Bolivarian Democracy: Participation, Politics and Culture under Chávez*. Durham. NC: Duke University Press, 2011.

Jones, Bart. *Hugo! The Hugo Chávez Story, from Mud Hut to Perpetual Revolution*. Hanover, NH: Steerforth Press, 2007.

Karl, Terry Lynn. *The Paradox of Plenty: Oil Booms and Petro-States*. Berkeley: University of California Press, 1997.

McCoy, Jennifer L., and Meyers, David J., eds. *The Unraveling of Representative Democracy in Venezuela*. Baltimore: John Hopkins University Press, 2006.

Ochoa, Marcia. *Queen for a Day: Transformistas, Beauty Queens, and the Performance of Femininity in Venezuela*. Durham, NC: Duke University Press, 2014.

Rabe, Stephen. *The Road to OPEC: United States Relations with Venezuela, 1919–1976*. Austin: University of Texas Press, 1982.

Tinker Salas, Miguel. *The Enduring Legacy: Oil, Culture, and Society in Venezuela*. Durham, NC: Duke University Press, 2009.

Tunstall, Tricia. *Changing Lives: Gustavo Dudamel, El Sistema, and the Transformative Power of Music*. New York: W. W. Norton, 2012.

Velasco, Alejandro. *Barrio Rising: Urban Popular Politics and the Making of Modern Venezuela*. Berkeley: University of California Press, 2015.

Wright, Winthrop R. *Café con Leche: Race, Class, and National Image in Venezuela*. Austin: University of Texas Press, 1990.

Wilpert, Gregory. *Changing Venezuela by Taking Power: The History and Policies of the Chavez Government*. London: Verso, 2007.

Yarrington, Doug. *A Coffee Frontier: Land, Society and Politics in Duaca, Venezuela, 1830–1936*. Pittsburgh: University of Pittsburgh Press, 1997.

Zahler, Reuben. *Ambitious Rebels: Remaking Honor, Law, and Liberalism in Venezuela, 1780–1850*. Tucson: University of Arizona Press, 2013.

INDEX